'This is a book filled with hope. Far from accepting the myth of inevitability, Brian Murphy dares us to imagine a just future in which ordinary people accept the mantle of "intentional citizenship" and create a moral alternative to economic globalization. Read this wonderful book.'
Maude Barlow, Chairperson, Council of Canadians

'This is such a hopeful, liberating book. One feels inspired to imagine something more transforming in our individual and collective lives as activists. It takes us to the edge of what we do not know. What an affirming place to arrive at.'
Lance Evoy, Coordinator, Institute in Management and Community Development, Concordia University

'Brian Murphy's *Transforming Ourselves, Transforming the World* is a wake-up call for the human spirit. For those lulled into inaction by hopelessness and fatalism, Murphy implores us to break out of our self-imposed limitations and recognize our vast potential for growth and change. Readers will undoubtedly be inspired to accept his enticing invitation to "subvert and conspire" in the name of social justice.'
Medea Benjamin, Co-director of Global Exchange, author of *Bridging the Global Gap*

'Brian Murphy's book provides a framework, in fact, almost a map, for those of us who "do believe, deep in our hearts, we shall overcome, some day". "Must" reading for all social justice activists.'
Kim Klein, author of *Fundraising for Social Change*, publisher of the Grassroots Fundraising Journal

'If you are disoriented, dispirited, or simply worn down by the enormity of it all, then curl up with the time-tested wisdom of Brian Murphy as he opens door after door into the miraculous world of social activism.'
John Cavanagh, Director, Institute for Policy Studies, Co-author, *Global Dreams: Imperial Corporations and the New World Order*

About the Author

Brian Murphy has for the past two decades worked for Inter Pares, an independent Canadian social justice and human rights organization, both in the field and at its headquarters in Ottawa. His present duties focus on policy development and programme support for Inter Pares' work in Asia, Africa, Latin America and Canada. He also chairs the governing body of the Project Counselling Service, an international NGO based in Costa Rica, which provides support to organizations working with people displaced by violence and repression in Latin America. In addition, he is a member of the Board of Advisors of the Institute in Management and Community Development, Concordia University, Montreal.

An educationalist particularly interested in international adult education, Brian Murphy began his career as a literacy specialist at Conestoga College, Kitchener, Ontario. After two years as a CUSO cooperant in West Africa (1968–70), he became Program Coordinator for Adult Basic Education at Algonquin College in Ottawa before joining the staff of Inter Pares. He is the author of numerous articles on development and Third World issues. This is his first book.

Transforming Ourselves, Transforming the World

An Open Conspiracy for Social Change

BRIAN K. MURPHY

ZED BOOKS
London & New York

INTER PARES
Ottawa

FERNWOOD PUBLISHING
Halifax, Nova Scotia

Transforming Ourselves, Transforming the World: An Open Conspiracy for Social Change was first published by
Zed Books Ltd, 7 Cynthia Street, London N1 9JF, UK,
and Room 400, 175 Fifth Avenue, New York, NY 10010, USA in 1999

in association with
Inter Pares, 58 Arthur Street, Ottawa, Canada K1R 7B9

Published in Canada by Fernwood Publishing Ltd,
PO Box 9409, Station A, Halifax, Nova Scotia, Canada B3K 5S3

Distributed in the USA exclusively by St Martin's Press, Inc.,
175 Fifth Avenue, New York, NY 10010, USA

Copyright © Brian K. Murphy 1999

The right of Brian K. Murphy to be identified as the author of this
work has been asserted by him in accordance with the Copyright,
Designs and Patents Act, 1988

Typeset in Monotype Garamond by Lucy Morton & Robin Gable, Grosmont
Cover designed by Andrew Corbett
Printed and bound in the United Kingdom
by Biddles Ltd, Guildford and King's Lynn

A catalogue record for this book is available from the British Library

Library of Congress Cataloging-in-Publication Data
Murphy, Brian K., 1944–
    Transforming ourselves, transforming the world : an open
conspiracy for social change / Brian K. Murphy.
        p.   cm.
    Includes bibliographical references.
    ISBN 1–85649–706–2 (hbk.). — ISBN 1–85649–707–0 (pbk.)
        1. Social change.   2. Social action.   3. Commitment
(Psychology).   4. Political activists—Psychology.   I. Title.
HM831.M87   1999
303.4—dc 21   99–20786
                                                                            CIP

Canadian Cataloguing in Publication Data
Murphy, Brian K., 1944–
    Transforming ourselves, transforming the world
    Includes bibliographical references and index.
    ISBN 1–55266–013–3
        1. Community development.   2. Social action.   I. Title.
HM831.M87   1999
361.7   C99–950124–0

ISBN 1 85649 706 2 (Hb)
ISBN 1 85649 707 0 (Pb)
ISBN 1 55266 013 3 (Canada)

Contents

This book is dedicated to my sons, Gaelan and Devin
in memory of
Myrna Mack Chang

We have no guarantee that humanity is not an aberration of evolution, a doomed sideline. At most we can only be an experiment, a possibility in the process. Consciousness has given us the power to destroy ourselves as well as the power to preserve ourselves. Nothing shows more clearly that to be human is not a privilege, but an irrelevance to all except humanity.

John Fowles, *The Aristos*

We are nature's unique experiment to make the rational intelligence prove itself sounder than the reflex. Knowledge is our destiny. Self-knowledge, at last bringing together the experience of the arts, and the explanation of science, waits ahead of us.

Jacob Bronowski, *The Ascent of Man*

Preface and Acknowledgements

We live in difficult times. The world is a bleak and barren place for so many of its people, and sometimes it looks as though everything decent and splendid that people once dreamed about creating in human society was merely a false hope, now lost for ever. Certainly the best traditions of social solidarity have been temporarily routed by the prophets of the marketplace and – in the industrialized nations no less than the countries of the South – we have seen the precipitous withdrawal of the state and government from the historic responsibility of caring for its citizens and promoting the general welfare of society, whether in health, education and employment, or in more general issues such as urban development, food security, rural transformation, and the protection of local economies.

Many of us who have been politically and socially active all our lives are faced with the disheartening prospect of seeing most of the gains made in a lifetime lost in one generation, and the opportunities for the young diminished beyond imagination. Many who are still active are discouraged, and many more on the brink of political engagement wonder, 'What is the point?', and turn away disheartened and isolated. For the new generation itself, growing up in these heartless times means, for many, growing up in the face of what now seem like mere illusions and false promises, without the hope and social vision that inspired social movements thirty or sixty or ninety years ago. Indeed, for many young people, it is politics itself that has fallen into disrepute – the politics of their parents' generation, and indeed of the entire twentieth century with its terrible violence, destruction, decadence and corruption. The political world they experience daily is a cynical, corrupt and unprincipled landscape that repels and disgusts them, and they want no part of this politics, or the rhetoric that justifies it.

Still, in our own countries, and in every single country around the world, there are millions of women and men, young and old, who continue – in the face of setbacks, political alienation and the shadow of despair – to dedicate their lives to a profound and hopeful activism. These activists continue to come together to promote healthy communities where they live and work, struggling to create democratic economies and accountable government, fighting for economic and social justice for all citizens, and demonstrating for peace and human rights in their own countries and internationally. They struggle together to improve their lives and the lives of their neighbours, and to keep alive a dream of a world based on the human values they have defined for themselves, a world which, at the very least, promises to strive continually towards one standard of dignity and opportunity for all citizens, regardless of who they are or where they live.

This activism is driven by necessity, and by the personal integrity, dignity and courage of millions of individual citizens working together to make their world a better place. But at the same time this activism is increasingly inhibited, and too often extinguished – particularly among the young – by the inevitable conclusion that change, fundamental change, will never be achieved in the face of the globalized power and greed and authoritarianism of the elites who have come to control the world we share.

This book examines, and attempts to transcend, this conclusion. It focuses on human capacities and the possibility of bringing about substantive change in ourselves and the world we share. Its antecedents are in existentialism and critical theory, liberationist education (see the work of Paulo Freire), and New Left 'third force' social psychology – all currents that are somewhat *passé* these days, but which we would all benefit from seeing revived.

Most political theorists do not deal with the psychosocial, whereas that is where this book begins. I would like to think that it is a good companion to the likes of Noam Chomsky and his colleagues, or John Pilger. Commentators like Pilger and Chomsky provide an invaluable service to the cause of justice and humanity, as they describe the world relentlessly and accurately, building a case for fundamental resistance and change action. Their books make readers ask, 'What can I do?' But many feel guilty as they do nothing at all, or feel insignificant in their tentative small actions. This book deals with the significance of action, and the fundamental question of whether and how progressive change is possible. And in particular, it situates the role of transformative knowledge in the change process.

The outline for this book emerges from my own praxis as an international activist for over thirty years – as an organizer and a leader of activist organizations, as an activist scholar, as an educator, as a writer. The book is the result of all these activities, and reflects and synthesizes these experiences. I have developed the ideas in the book in my work over several years, and have tested various parts of it in seminars with community-level activists, and specifically with multigenerational groups of activists, most recently through the Summer Program of the Institute in Community Development at Concordia University in Montreal. I have reorganized and reworked the text as a result of using the content in seminars at Concordia. It was the response of seminar participants to the substance of the material that convinced me to try to get it published.

Part I begins with an introductory chapter that introduces and outlines the rationale and central ideas of the book. In Chapter 2 I describe in more detail the social and personal dilemmas that we face as activists and potential activists, dilemmas that prevent action for change. These dilemmas are analysed from the perspective of sanity and health, defined as physical and spiritual wholeness. An interplay between stress, anxiety, alienation, isolation and perceived impotence and helplessness is analysed as a 'psychology of inertia' which inhibits creativity and action. Chapter 3, then, is a practical discussion of how we can begin to confront this inertia to envision another way and another world and, with others, bring our vision to the world in concrete action. The concept of 'humanist radicalism' is introduced and explained, and the possibility of building an open conspiracy for social change is introduced.

In Part II I examine human beings and human society as open-ended 'possibilities in process'. Chapter 4 provides an analysis of the essential qualities and capacities that embody the potential of each of us to transcend the conditions of our lives and change the world. Human beings are presented as a potential 'missing link' between a deterministic past and an intentional and conscious future. Chapter 5 explores individual consciousness and social identity as critical variables in human social development. The nature of knowledge is analysed as a determining factor in action. The qualities of consciousness and 'vision' – our capacity to see what is, and imagine what is not yet, but could be – are highlighted as central to activism and change. The social quality of individual action is analysed. In Chapter 6, several impediments to transformative consciousness and vision are analysed as inherent within conventional rationality. Central to this analysis is a critique of the concepts of immutable human nature and a static, deterministic natural law. The need to confront fatalism, and challenge the mechanistic and deterministic paradigm which explains and justifies the prevailing human condition, is established. Chapter 7 then offers a comprehensive descriptive analysis of the type of education that would nurture authentic human learning and consciousness and the capacity for lifelong critical and responsible social action. It defines the political goal of a 'democracy of the intellect', and is a prescription for education as praxis, for praxis, through praxis.

In Part III I explore more fully the possibility of an 'open conspiracy' for social change, locally and globally. In Chapter 8, the idea of open conspiracy is elaborated in concrete terms as an open, public and broad-based proposition to transform elements of the prevailing social order, linking the discussion directly back to Chapters 2 and 3. The concepts of 'reference groups' and 'action groups' are introduced and explained as the practical forms of initial localized 'conspiracy'. In Chapter 9, a tentative model for developing the basis for local conspiracy is offered by elaborating four progressive and cumulative 'theatres' of reflection and action which confront inertia and begin to build the mutual support necessary to sustain action and build a conspiracy. Chapter 10 then discusses the central place and role of (formal and informal) learning and education in open conspiracy. Development education (long out of vogue in social justice activism) is redefined as knowledge and action for social change and development – rather than merely education about 'development' – and analysed as a potential unifying construct to consolidate the philosophy, focus and the initial strategy of an open conspiracy. This chapter promotes a strategy of confronting dominant social and political paradigms by asserting propositional 'facts-in-action' that challenge conventional wisdom and subvert local and global practices of inhumanity and exploitation, while building participation and the scope of the open conspiracy.

The main text is concluded with a brief personal reflection on the writing of the book, and as a counterpoint to the sustained treatise of the main text I have included an epilogue which offers a range of short reflections, some from my personal journal of years as an activist, others from writers who have influenced my praxis – each of which is an interlude or a vignette that resonates with the ethical and aesthetic impulse that drives the book.

Before acknowledging some of the people who, through their own activism, have helped me to bring this book to life, I want to say a word about the quotations from other writers that are used throughout the text. Many of these excerpts use the word 'man', and the pronoun 'he', when referring to people in general, or to all of us as humankind, and in other ways reflect a gender-biased perspective in their diction. At one point in preparing this text I considered editing these quotes to make them gender inclusive, and soon discovered that this was a fruitless – indeed, dishonest – exercise. Trying to plaster it over by editing and ellipsis merely obscured what we all know – that much of what we read, even if it is written by progressive thinkers, contains this bias, which is an affront. I finally decided that in general (there are exceptions, where the edit is obvious) I would leave the quotations in their original, while trying to use a more inclusive pattern in my own writing. I leave the reader to judge the merits of the choices I have made.

This book is dedicated to the memory of Myrna Mack Chang, whose life as an activist scholar and human rights advocate in Guatemala embodied the kind of commitment and heroism that are required by those of us who want to participate in a just and humane transformation of the world. Myrna openly and courageously defied the murderous oligarchy and military machine in Guatemala to document and publicize internationally the long campaign of terror and genocide they conducted against the Mayan peasants of her country. For this crime against them, on the night of 11 September 1990, they came out of the shadows and savagely cut Myrna down in the street, two blocks from the National Palace in downtown Guatemala City. Although Myrna's final sacrifice will be required of few of us, it is our obligation to continue to bear witness to her life and struggle

– and that of thousands of other martyrs to justice – and to see, as far as possible, that others will not have to suffer her death. It is in this spirit that this book is written, and I am forever indebted to the inspiration that Myrna played in my life in the very brief time that I knew her.

A few words about others whose lives and struggle are an intimate part of the process that led to this book. The concept of an 'open conspiracy', as I elaborate it, emerged in the late 1970s as a result of work and discussions with several people then working in community development and adult education in Ottawa and Montreal – among others, Guy Coté, who introduced me to the concept, Ruth Baldwin, Mike Kelly, Lindy Tierney, Lance Evoy, Brian Rowe and Jean Christie. When I first began to collect these thoughts together in early 1979, Ruth Baldwin in particular was very helpful and supportive in bringing a critical eye to my fledgling effort to draft what twenty years later has emerged, in a much different form, as the present book. Since then the ideas have evolved in my work within the Inter Pares team, and I am forever indebted to the close conspiracy that I have had with my many friends and colleagues at Inter Pares over twenty years. They are too many to mention, but all of you know who you are, and I am forever grateful for the encouragement and support that you have offered in getting this book published.

As part of my work within Inter Pares, the constant collaboration with Lance Evoy – first at the Third Avenue Resource Centre, and later at the Institute in Community Development at Concordia University – has been an inspiration and a constant learning laboratory about community change activism. Lance's encouragement was greatly instrumental in forcing me back to my desk to try to put this book together, and his critical comments during the drafting were invaluable.

In my work in Latin America I have learned much from the work and accompaniment of several dear friends over many years, especially Ana Eugenia Marín, Diana Avila, Gladys Acosta, Johanna Aberle, Frances Arbour and Gordon Hutchison, who, in their tireless actions, have exemplified the commitment and artistry possible in nurturing popular processes to promote human rights, economic justice and social transformation in the Americas. In Europe, Herman van Aken, Alfred Fritschi and Pia Poulsen have also been invaluable friends and colleagues in their untiring commitment to generating resources and political solidarity for our joint work in support of popular struggles for justice in Latin America.

Over this period of almost twenty years, collaboration with and mutual support from Sergio Aguayo – not least our regular long walks and far-ranging conversations – have been treasured moments to reflect and test reality around our common cause and shared activism – in Canada, in Mexico, and in the rest of the Americas – and have influenced the direction of this book.

The courage and capacity to engage in this work originally, and to continue regardless of the early trials, is a gift I owe to my lifelong friend, Rose Mary Murphy, who accompanied me through some of my darkest hours and earliest adventures. It is with and through Rose Mary that I first encountered and struggled to internalize feminist theory and practice, and the fundamental truth of the unity of the personal and the political. Rose Mary's commitment to transformative processes in both her teaching and her community activism is living testimony to many of the propositions in this book, and has in part inspired them.

The fact that this book has finally seen the light of day in a readable form is in no small part due to the assistance I have received from my close friend and colleague Jean Symes, with whom I have enjoyed a deep and shared praxis over the ten years of our collaboration. Among other things, through our shared work Jean has helped me to learn how to write all over again. Her extensive critical comments on successive drafts of this book – both its form and its content – contributed invaluably to the extent that whatever lies before you is clear, accessible and useful to frontline activists.

Finally, my kids, Gaelan and Devin, allowed me to live again my childhood, and now my adulthood, through fresh and healthier eyes. Their constant commentary on the parade – the world and the living of life – continues to help me question and requestion the assumptions on which I live and act. I am forever grateful, and they bring me constant pleasure and joy, even in the hardest times. This book is for them, and for all the young people who are just beginning now to embrace the future that we are creating together.

Brian Murphy

Part I

The Challenge

But the final cure is not in his past-dissecting fingers
But in a future of action, the will and the fist
Of those who abjure the luxury of self-pity
And prefer to risk a movement without being sure
If movement would be better or worse in a hundred
Years or a thousand when their heart is pure.
None of our hearts are pure, we always have mixed motives
Are self-deceivers, but the worst of all
Deceits is to murmur 'Lord, I am not worthy'
And, lying easy, turn your face to the wall.
But may I cure that habit, look up and outwards
And may my feet follow my wider glance
First no doubt to stumble, then to walk with others
And in the end – with time and luck – to dance.

Louis MacNeice, from *Autumn Journal 'III'*

1

The Courage to Be

We are in for a very, very long haul ... I am asking for everything you have to give. We will never give up.... You will lose your youth, your sleep, your patience, your sense of humour and occasionally, the understanding and support of people who love you very much. In return, I have nothing to offer you but your pride in being a woman, and all your dreams you've ever had for your daughters and nieces and granddaughters ... and the certain knowledge that at the end of your days you will be able to look back and say that once in your life you gave everything you had for justice.

Jill Ruckelshaus

A central dilemma of contemporary activism is despair and political disorientation. While incredibly good and courageous work is being done by millions of social activists around the world, in the North and the South, many are expressing a loss of hope and direction and, with the devaluation of classical ideological paradigms, there is a corresponding vacuum in progressive social theory on which to base change action.

This book addresses the fundamental question of change. It defines human beings as possibilities, *in process* – the process of becoming, of development, of change. The future for human society could be a brutal, miserable existence, as many currently predict,[1] but it could just as well be a creative, open and humane existence. The future is not determined; it is influenced by what we do now in our various communities, in our various countries, and in common cause internationally – by the possibilities we envision and the actions we take to make our visions reality.

This book is a proposition: a proposal for how individual people, and people in groups, can form a *conspiracy* – an open and public conspiracy – to begin to change the present and influence the future in a positive progressive direction; in fact, to influence the evolution of human society, and human beings themselves. When I use the word 'conspiracy' in this way, the first reaction is often confused, since people are used to conspiracy being a negative idea – implying secret, subversive, even treasonous behaviour. I am proposing that we reappropriate this word, and the very act of conspiring together, and transform it into a positive and transcendent form of social and political action. *Secret?* No. This is a conspiracy that is open, and defiant, and celebratory! *Subversive?* Yes. This would be a conspiracy that is publicly and explicitly subversive[2] of everything in society – systems, institutions and structures – that erodes humanity and individual dignity, and exploits people as though they were machines. *Treasonous?* Never. The conspiracy described in this book is the antithesis of treason – a conspiracy based on our full and open practice of responsible citizenship to hold accountable those who would use their privilege to betray the human values of equality, justice and social solidarity in the interests of greed and power.

When I speak of 'we' in this book, I am generally speaking of citizens, of whatever country or region, who are struggling to confront the structures that oppress them and others, and reduce their humanity and dignity. The book is addressed to fellow activists (or aspiring activists) and citizens of the world.

The book is clearly values-led, the values being peace, justice and dignity for all human beings. It relates directly to the reader, as an individual person, and her or his capacity to make choices and take action, with others. It presents action as the practice and maintenance of health – of being physically and spiritually whole and sane and alive – and explores why it is reasonable and worth it to act, even when individual acts may seem on the surface to have insignificant effect. At the same time, the book elaborates a framework for renewed action and learning – a 'political epistemology', if you like – that explains why positive, progressive social organization is not only possible, but natural; and it isolates some basic principles to promote such organization while resisting prevailing structures of repression and oppression. The book is written at both a personal and a theoretical level. It engages at the level of values, as well as intellect and politics. It elaborates what *could* be rather than merely what *should* be, and deals directly and practically with the individual inertia that prevents the first steps from which change movements build.

A friend from Mexico has talked with me about the need for a 'manual for the disorientated'. In fact, this book is not a handbook, since such a handbook is not really possible (recalling the irony of Georges Perec's brilliant novel *Life: A User's Manual*); but in another sense the comment resonates: some of the elements are there.

The book is not intended as a 'scholarly' work as such, although I have tried to ensure that it is internally rigorous and well-grounded. It is intended for activists and community organizers, and potential activists and organizers; for young adults and students who are looking for political orientation, and for lifelong activists for whom it may crystallize convictions and insights gained in a lifetime of struggle. I hope it will also be of interest to progressive educators, and to social theorists and scholars who see their role as activist intellectuals.

The book does not presume or require a formal background in social theory. And while it is written from a North American perspective, the themes it explores are not limited to the North American context; it elaborates a perspective on change action that is certainly applicable elsewhere, and is as relevant to social change processes in the South as in the North.

I focus on our personal experiences – on the private, as well as the public – because I believe that the private and personal realm is where community starts, and where struggle begins. This is the realm of our lives as activists to which we devote the least time, but it affects us the most. We are continually walking about with hundreds of other activists, all of us talking about struggle and change, yet we rarely share our *private* thoughts, the personal reality that moves us beyond ideals of struggle, or change, or justice, to transformative action. As we work together, we are joined by our common cause, by the work and issues we share, and by the discourse that we have adopted to share these issues. At the same time we are *separated* – by our private thoughts and experiences; by our personal dilemmas concerning life and the living of it; by the monologue that goes on in our head every day: the conversation that no one hears but ourselves.

It is imperative that we begin to share some of this experience, the *personal* of the political – this monologue that we never get an opportunity to share in an environment of trust and solidarity. Especially we need to create the opportunity to share the critical problem of optimism and despair. What problems and forces seem to be driving us to give up our dreams of making the world a better place, and what experiences help us to continue? What makes us want to quit and leave all this behind? And what sustains us to go at it for another day?

My work has been privileged by the fact that I have been able to be both a local activist where I live, in Canada, and, at the same time, an international activist in the wider world. In my Canadian activism my work originally focused on literacy and adult education, but quickly moved beyond this to focus on poverty, gender, race and class, and especially the rights of immigrants and refugees, and on human rights in general, conceived as the 'right to be' as a fully functioning human being and an active political and economic participant in society. This is also the focus of my international activism, which most recently has concentrated on the struggles against political repression and militarism in Latin America.

As a reformed high-school dropout, I started doing literacy work with unemployed factory workers in southern Ontario in the mid-1960s, then landed in West Africa in 1968, living in Nigeria during the Biafran crisis, just in time to watch the legacy of colonialism begin its tragic and bloody unravelling. In almost thirty years of this work, I have many times faced the prospect of quitting.

There were many moments when I considered leaving activism behind and finding a more quiet and tranquil life away from the pressure of community. The pivotal crisis was some fifteen years ago, when I was in my late thirties. If I was ever to quit, that was probably the moment – not because I was faced with how bad the world was, but because I was faced with how inadequate my friends and I were to the task of social activism and solidarity with the poor and most marginal people in our community. I could no longer avoid the implication that a major barrier to social change was ourselves – that we simply did not have the will and the determination, the faith, to do what was necessary to confront greed and violence.

The specific issue was a literacy programme that we had started. But the real issue was the divisions within our group about methods, about priorities, about power, about politics and public profile, and personality. We talked endlessly about literacy and poverty, and about social change, but our practice with the participants in the programme was little different from our practice when some of us had worked together at the local community college. And the internal jealousy and tensions within our group were destroying even our capacity to function at all. Ultimately, the group did split, several people left the organization, and those who remained struggled on doing some good work, but the heart and passion that had marked the first years of the project had been destroyed. I was left with anger at what had happened, and the loss of some good friends.

But I also experienced a terrible resolve: it would be easier to die than to quit. In fact, to quit would feel like dying. But I also knew that if nothing else in our work mattered, if we were to be able to stay alive and passionate, we had to love each other, to tell the truth to each other, and be critical of our own actions. And if we were serious about our work, we had to stop making 'the poor' the object of it, and engage with people as mutual subjects of our own lives and history. It is from this resolve that this book has emerged. Its under-lying assumption is that human beings are creative agents capable of forming our own future and destiny. We can *choose to change*, and act on this choice to create the world we want.

The UNDP's *Human Development Report* establishes approximately two billion as the number of people living in absolute poverty in the world, North and South; these are human beings living on the very margin of existence with totally inadequate food, shelter, education, and health care.[3] Of these individuals, fully 66 per cent suffer from chronic malnutrition, 'the day-in, day-out, erosion of health that lack of food causes'. It is officially estimated that over fifteen million children under the age of five years die every year as the direct result of malnutrition. This figure probably does not reflect neo-natal mortality. Although the fact that one in every four children are dead by the age of five years is gruesome in itself, those children who survive are also affected, and it is estimated that over five hundred million human beings in the 'third' world are permanently physically and/or mentally diminished by malnutrition. This phenomenon is not limited to countries in the South – Asia, Africa and Latin America – it is also increasingly prevalent in the industrialized nations as the gap between rich and poor reaches levels not seen since the Indus-trial Revolution. We are seeing a true globalization of disparity, where all nations, North and South, are supporting a growing but still small and obscenely affluent professional elite, while the poorest become poorer and more alienated from society. In Canada, this growing underclass has reached a solid 20 per cent of the population, and, according to the government's own definitions, almost 25 per cent of Canadian children are living in permanent poverty.[4]

What are the prospects? An irony lies in the fact that, by and large, most Third World nations were still food self-sufficient in the 1950s. The UNDP reports that despite the enormous global economic growth of the past fifteen years, during this period the standard of living in the seventy countries where the poorest of the poor are concentrated has actually fallen in relative and absolute terms. In the quarter-century since 1975, the economic share of the poorest 20 per cent of the world's population – well over 1.5 billion people – has dropped to only 1.4 per cent from an already meagre 2.3 per cent. Current attitudes and practices on the part of the techno-scientifically advanced nations are not bringing about solutions to this economic disparity, and the indications are that unless attitudes and economic practices change – unless the concepts of human development, growth and value are transformed, and an ethic of radical global interdependence emerges – the human misery that will unfold will be cataclysmic.

Of course it is impossible to speak of mass human misery in meaningful terms. We talk of *future* cataclysm when for millions living today, life *is* cataclysm, life is unspeakable misery. The atrocities perpetrated on humans by humans in recent history seemingly cannot be outdone. Yet every time we conclude that we have witnessed the quintessential cruelty and callousness, another atrocity is committed that tests our tolerance for horror and our understanding of what it is to be human. The agony of the child bathed in liquid fire, smothered in 'defoliant', or emaciated by starvation and thirst; the outraged terror and impotence of the victim strapped broken to the torturer's rack or facing his ovens; the impenetrable sorrow of individuals forced to stand by powerlessly and witness the agony of loved ones, and even forced to wield the knife themselves – this damned anguish, the daily experience of millions, cannot be represented to those of us who are so incredibly fortunate to be temporarily insulated from these realities.

Misery and violent outrage are norms of human existence. Humans are engaged in constant warfare. Political incarceration, torture and execution are practised as a matter of course in scores of countries throughout the world. Cruel repression of human freedom on ideological, racial or religious grounds is a constitutional fact in many nations. And all this is a mere overlay, an added dimension to the gross disparities in quality of life between the so-called rich and poor nations, and within each of these nations themselves, rich and poor.

One thing is clear: the present situation will not persist. One very real possibility is that the entire globe, including the minority in the North and South favoured by the aberration of affluence, will be sucked into a vortex of human misery, moving to the crescendo of squalid and violent debasement of human potential predicted by commentators such as Robert Kaplan, whose long and vivid essay on 'The Coming Anarchy' in the November 1994 *Atlantic Monthly* (where Kaplan is Associate Editor) was a watershed in what has become a flood of material popularizing the bleak and breathtakingly ethnocentric viewpoint of the US foreign policy establishment. Or – and this is the possibility I wish to explore in this book – the global situation will improve: not by chance, but by the active, critical choice of millions of individuals to transform their lives and their societies to ensure global interdependence and justice, and the free expression of human potential.

This is the challenge. This is the imperative for human survival. Is it possible? Yes. The potential is there. We have the capacity to work this 'miracle'. Will it happen? There is considerable basis for hope. We do have the *capacity* to solve these problems. I do not know whether we have the will or the wisdom to translate our capacities into capabilities and, beyond that, to translate our capabilities into transforming *action*. But I think that we can, and that we will.

This book presents a paradigm for change action within a loose framework of what Erich Fromm (1970) has called 'humanist radicalism'. I explore our human capacities and suggest some strategies that might be useful in helping each of us to initiate the transforming actions that are demanded by our times. The book begins with the question, 'How do we move from dilemma, despair and inertia to gain, or regain, the dynamism of active humanist radicalism?' Our constant crisis as activists is the danger of becoming 'burnt-out', of losing energy and the will to act: conscious in our intellect, but so immersed in our own reality that we cannot act, so alienated from our sisters and brothers that we cannot speak, so oppressed by what is that we can no longer hope for what could be. We internalize the human condition rather than externalize our own vision. We see our significance not in who we are and what we do, but from what is, and from what effect we produce on what is. And we are burnt-out, we are resigned, we have despaired.

To confront this inertia we need to assert in practice ideas that contradict the irrational in today's society, to initiate new modes of human expression and new perceptions of human potential. And we need to do so not because such initiatives will bring utopia, but because inaction is insane and suicidal. We choose not to 'escape our freedom' but, rather, to *practise* freedom; this very act is the essence of humanness.

Our first step is not to decide whether our action will result in a new world but, rather, to decide that our consciousness must result in action *regardless*, whatever the eventual outcome. We liberate ourselves from our own psychology of inertia and fatalism. We defeat the sense of personal futility and nothingness. In Herbert Marcuse's (1964) terms, we move past the one-dimensionality of our perceptions – the tendency to see only what is – and promote the second dimension of perception: seeing what is not – and, therefore, what might be. We allow ourselves the liberty of 'insanity' – the ability to define the irrational character of the established rationality; and of 'negative thinking' – critique, contradiction, transcendence. In Paulo Freire's (1970) terms, we see beyond our 'limit-situations' to 'untested feasibilities', articulated in dialogue.

This book proposes the development of an open conspiracy, based in the approach of humanist radicalism. I will argue that we can conspire together to transform our sociocultural reality, and we can proclaim our conspiracy to our society at large, professing our conviction that there are better ways, bearing witness to the potential of the human individual, asserting the fundamental need and right for every person to practise freedom. We can publicly confront the established order with critiques of current practice and with alternative feasibilities. We can practise an open conspiracy of women and men in free authorship of our own futures, and present our conspiracy publicly, as a new fact, a new discourse, a contradiction in dynamic interaction with the established 'fact' and the dominant discourse of competition and control. If we can do this, we can begin to re-create real health – physical and spiritual wholeness and sanity – for ourselves and others. There will be transformations in society. There will be new beginnings towards social justice. And we will be alive.

Not so very long after the events that led to my moment of anger and near-despair described earlier, I had another experience – one that was more lyrical, but which relates similarly to the issue of resolve and will. It is a moment I carry with me to this day, a small flame that helps me to resist despair no matter what else tugs at and tatters my dreams.

I was in El Salvador in the mid-1980s, one of many, many visits I made to that country during its terrible civil war, visits that brought me to the edge of hope and faith in humanity. I travelled often in the countryside across the invisible lines that marked the zones controlled by the army and the guerrilla forces of the FMLN, faced continuously with the tragedy of this struggle and the violence that the people suffered. It was very easy to be overwhelmed by the sheer inhumanity of it all, and the seeming hopelessness of the cause.

One day I was in a small *asentamiento* – a settlement for displaced people whose agricultural projects we were funding. We were walking about and came upon a family of women in their humble adobe-and-straw home. It was early evening, and the sun was setting on this little group: an old, old woman, who might easily have been a hundred; her daughter, almost seventy; *her* daughter, the old woman's granddaughter, who was in her mid-thirties; and a teenage girl, about sixteen, the new generation. A mother, a daughter, a granddaughter, and a great-granddaughter. Four generations of struggle in one circle.

I must have looked very, very serious, and humourless, because the women laughed and chided me, and asked me why I was visiting them if I had nothing to say. Then the old woman told me that I should relax and enjoy the evening with them, and stop my frowning. 'Don't feel sorry for us,' she said: 'We are alive, and we will survive. You are welcome to be with us, but only if you can enjoy our place with us and see what there is to celebrate in our simple lives.'

'Are you happy?', she then asked. I responded that I didn't think so; what was there to be happy about? She replied that if she had what I had, she would be very happy, and would enjoy it every day. 'Do not be ashamed of what you have,' she said. 'Enjoy it! That is what you owe to us. To enjoy, and then to share your joy with us. We do not need your sadness, or your shame.'

We had quite a conversation then – about home, and family, and children, and the war, and struggle. But the beginning of the conversation will always be with me: a gift, a lesson, offered to me, who had so much, from an old woman who had so little, but who had more to give than I could have imagined until I met her. From that day I was pledged whenever I felt despair to defeat it with a celebration of the life I had, and the courage to be, and to live, that she had shown me. Her gift was a gift of life.

This is the real meaning of struggle, and if we have the wisdom and the will, we can sustain each other by celebrating ourselves, and the struggle – personal and political – that defines our being and our lives.

Notes

1. See Robert Kaplan's epic and remarkably influential essay, 'The Coming Anarchy', *Atlantic Monthly*, November 1994; or Samuel Huntington's *The Clash of Civilizations and the New World Order* (1996, 1998), the prevailing bible of *realpolitik* within the foreign policy establishment in the United States.
2. See *Teaching as a Subversive Activity* (1969), a delightful and influential little book by Neil Postman and Charles Weingartner that put a liberating structure to the best instincts of a generation of young progressive educators in North America, and could serve the next generation as well, in North America and beyond; it focuses especially on ways to help students learn to understand the treachery of official language, and detect bullshit (the authors call it 'crap-detecting').
3. See United Nations Development Program (UNDP), *Human Development Report* 1988, United Nations/Oxford University Press, 1998.
4. See *A Human Rights Meltdown in Canada*, submission of the National Anti-Poverty Organization (NAPO) to the UN Committee on Economic, Social and Cultural Rights, on the occasion of the consideration of Canada's Third Report on the Implementation of the International Covenant on Economic, Social and Cultural Rights, Geneva, November 1998.

2

The Dilemma of Action
and the Psychology of Inertia

I cannot recall a time ... when there was so much talk about the individual's capacities and potentialities and so little actual confidence on the part of the individual about his power to make a difference psychologically or politically.

Rollo May, *Power and Innocence*

It is not news that the world must be changed, and not so very radical to suggest that change can come only from the action of each one of us. But how can it happen? How do we choose? How do we act? How can we change – even as individuals, let alone as societies and ultimately as a global society?

In trying to respond to this question, the most pressing problem arises in the form of a dilemma. Most of the determining factors for the human condition – material, intellectual, 'spiritual' – lie rooted in society itself. How can a society initiate and promote a change process that represents the very antithesis of the prevailing ethos of that society, and its complex of social structures, norms, institutions and culture? Where do we start?

Even if the consciousness necessary for basic social change were relatively widespread – and it *is* far more widespread than is commonly acknowledged – it is extremely difficult to transfer this awareness into direct social action for basic change, when society does not contain within it structures through which basic change can be effected – indeed, when the dominant structures in all societies actually *impede* basic change and reflect, maintain, protect and promote the obedience, docility and fatalism that preserve the status quo.

This is a major dilemma. When we face it squarely – especially after many failed attempts to 'change things' – a very common response is hopelessness. It appears too big. The conclusion for many of us who experience this defeat and despair is that true democracy is impossible, and social equity and justice are a dream. And we feel compelled to insulate ourselves from reality, and retreat within the very small domain that we can control, to seek security, comfort and peace of mind at least there.

This instinct for self-preservation is understandable. But another response *is* possible. It comes from an analysis of a second fundamental problem in change dynamics: human psychology – specifically, what I will call *the psychology of inertia*.

The dilemma we have just described, concerning the apparent impossibility of effecting fundamental social change in an unjust world, is an extrinsic dilemma; it is an analysis of an *external* reality. The psychosomatic response of despair and inertia that this analysis – and the real situation it describes – creates in the individual is an intrinsic dilemma; it is an *internal* reality. Social change is impeded not only by the extrinsic dilemma of social reality – which, in fact, is precisely what we seek to change; it is critically impeded also by the *intrinsic* dilemma of individual despair and perceived powerlessness, and the concurrent psychology of inertia. Just as the activist individual is the critical agent of social change, so the individual, rendered powerless and inert, is a critical barrier to social change.

Most of us, when faced with the experience we have been discussing, pose a question to ourselves: 'I live in an irrational world bent on self-destruction; how do I act to change this world?' This formulation focuses on the external, and underscores our individual powerlessness. But suppose we frame the problem another way: 'I am dissatisfied with the world and my relation with it; how do I act to become satisfied?' This is a more powerful and useful formulation. It is self-centred, focusing on self rather than on some objective – and overwhelming – fault with the world.

This shift in the way the problem is perceived is significant because it contains an implicit premiss: *all action is 'selfish', directed towards achieving or maintaining health.* By health I mean the state of an organism in which all its aspects are fully integrated and functioning at their individual and collective potential. The organism – an entity more than the collection of its aspects – is whole and functioning in an optimal manner (the word 'health' originally meant 'well' or 'whole'), in that its capacity for interaction with its world is actualized and practised. In this context the problem can now be posed: 'The world is unhealthy, and I am unhealthy with/in it. How do I act to achieve health, and to maintain it?'

The factors that prevent my becoming an agent of change lie in my psychology as well as in my society. Since my psychology – hopelessness, despair, fear, 'paralysis of will' – prevents even individual, personal movement, it is there that *I* must start. The powers of the status quo know this, and direct much more attention to maintaining a 'psychology of inertia' than they do to constructing structural barriers to change. Therefore we need to begin to resolve the dilemma of action by directing our attention to our personal psychology of inertia, and then to our inertia as a group. To this end we also need to explore the phenomena of dilemma, choice and action in the context of health and motivation, because the dilemmas are, essentially, dilemmas of personal health and survival; and our choices and actions are, essentially, assertions of a commitment to health.

To explore the dilemma of action from this perspective, the starting point is the premiss that all action is ultimately 'selfish' – that is, 'self'-centred – and aimed at maintaining or achieving health. The elements we want to examine are the factors that promote or inhibit health in the individual, the prevailing threats to individual health and, finally, alternative responses to 'unhealth'.

Factors in Health[1]

Security

The first factor in health is *security of existence*. Basically, the elements of security are self-evident: freedom from crippling or fatal disease (physical well-being), possession of the basic materials for sustenance (maintaining physical well-being), comfort consistent with prevailing expectations within the social milieu, and the confidence that physical well-being and comfort are not under imminent threat.

Health depends upon the satisfaction of needs, 'real' and perceived. Even in the realm of material and physical security there is a subjective, relative element based on our expectations and perceptions of the adequacy of our security, and how each of us measures changes in 'adequate security' in our actual situation on an ongoing basis. What leads to a feeling of security for one person may be a source of anxiety for another. The influence of this element of subjectivity varies according to the breadth of the line between security and disaster. A clear and present danger such as war, catastrophe, and ongoing civil or economic strife, or the perpetual hand-to-mouth existence common in much of the Third World and pervasive also among the hidden poor of industrialized society, significantly narrows the gap between the subjective and objective elements in security, although the subjective, relative element is always present. In this sense, health and material and physical security can be seen as a subjective and relative state as much as an objective, normative state, with the understanding that beyond a certain threshold of constant or temporary hazard, the distinction becomes largely academic.

Self-worth

A second factor in health is the perception of self-worth and the sanctity of self. This entails a balance between *ego* – my sense of self, unique and solitary – and *identity* – my sense of belonging to a group and being accepted as a useful member of that group. This balance is reflected in the relationship between what we know, believe, think and feel (what I will later refer to as 'vision') and how we act. If there is discord between what we believe and how we act, the result is unhealth, manifested in anxiety and alienation.

The root of the dissonance between our thoughts and our acts is most commonly a conflict between our need for acceptance of self by self, and our need for acceptance of self by others – a need that is often related to our need for material and social security. Health can thrive only when we are in a situation in which our actions can be consistent with our vision of self and the world. Unhealth becomes rampant when we are in a situation in which our actions must contradict – that is, 'speak against' – our vision of self and the world in order for us to be accepted by the group. In such situations the source of unhealth is twofold.

The first is obvious: discord between our thoughts and our deeds. The second is more subtle, and particularly ironic. The ultimate value of being accepted by others lies in our ego being in harmony with our identity – that is, our authentic, personal sense of self, as manifest in behaviour, being accepted by others. When we alter our behaviour to obtain acceptance, that acceptance is not of our real self but of a false, unknown, anti-self. Not only do we sacrifice authentic action, but we fail to receive acceptance of authentic self. We are in a double-bind, split-off from our real self. There is a contradiction between what we must do to nurture our ego – our internal sense of integrity of self; and what we must do to nurture our identity – our sense of being acceptable and of value to the group. This situation leads to a very real act of negation of self – in extreme terms, a type of spiritual suicide. The sanctity of self is destroyed; we are aliens both in our own 'inner space' and in the external world. This phenomenon is pervasive today, and it is a central malaise of society.

Related to this malaise is the matter of culture. Culture is the collective response of a group to its environment, a response which includes art, education, science and technology, religion, along with social norms and activities. The role of culture in the life of the individual is complex. On the one hand, the very process of individual development ensures that each of us will internalize, to a considerable extent, aspects of the culture of our group, especially in terms of world-view, perceptual sets, and behavioural patterns and expectations.

At the same time, in a very real sense each individual is a cultural unit who develops his or her own unique responses to the environment within the broader context of a sociocultural set. When our personal responses clash with the established responses of society as a whole, or of the more immediate local group of which we feel a part, there is a classic conflict between our ego and our identity – one made more perilous because of the formative role our parent culture has played in our self-development.

This phenomenon is pervasive in our societies, and becomes more and more prevalent as technological and economic developments bring about societal change at a pace much faster than the cultural group can respond to, and adapt, and modify. As a result, adaptation to societal change – a significant element of which is an explosive expansion of direct and vicarious experience, and of knowledge – becomes more and more an *individual* response and less and less a societal response. The potential for ego/identity conflict is dramatically heightened; the possibility for integrated responses by the larger group is dramatically diminished. A case in point is the common observation that existing mechanisms for changing or creating laws can no longer keep pace with rapidly changing social conditions and expectations.

Dealing with this relatively recent phenomenon in human development is a problem that each one of us – and every society and culture – faces. Any permanent solution will, of necessity, be more substantive than the present response, which lies essentially in tangential, subcultural (often 'cultic') spin-offs.

Creative life

A third factor in health is the practice of a creative life. This factor is closely related to the concepts of self-worth, sanctity and identity. By 'creative life' I mean a life which is predicated on action *with* the environment – including the community of human persons – to create meaningful and fruitful situations, rather than mere adaptations *to* the environment to avoid unpleasant situations. The creative life connotes that as individuals each of us is the author of our own life-acts, and the creator of the life-spaces we inhabit, and that this creativity is in harmony with our personal world-view. The creative life is formative as well as adaptive, active as well as reactive, directed 'towards' the environment as well as 'from' it, 'with' the environment as well as 'in' it. The individual is *creator* as well as *creature*.

Essential to the creative life is the practice of 'vision'. This involves 'seeing how things are', particularly how things are *for oneself* – creating our own knowledge and perception and relevance rather than merely absorbing or adopting a prescribed perception. In seeing how things are, vision also involves seeing 'how things are *not*'. And, finally, vision involves creating intention, 'seeing how things might be'. This is the person as visionary. The creative life is authentic authorship of self and reality, in harmony with one's vision of what might be possible.[2]

Integral to the creative life is the element of dialogue. As authors of our own life-acts and creators of life-space, we share our acts and our space with other people. Our authorship (authority) is shared. Our mode of action as authors, therefore, needs to include dialogue as a permanent strategy. We need an environment that both respects the sanctity of the individual, as author, and that promotes identity through authentic dialogue and mutuality of action within the community of authors. The creative life is one in which the individual works, with control over his or her personal life-forces, in harmony with capacities, aptitudes and personal vision, and in co-operative mutuality within his or her social group.

These, then, are the key factors in healthy human life: *security, self-worth* and individual *sanctity*, and the *creative life* characterized by *mutuality*. Central to the development and maintenance of health is the actualization of creative harmony between personal vision and behaviour.

Threats to Health

The most prevalent threat to our personal health is the inherent contradiction between our autonomy and sovereignty, and our social and material needs and expectations. Most immediately this is reflected in the tension and conflict between, on the one hand, our need to express authentic self and personal vision through action within a dynamic life and, on the other, society's fundamental tendency towards stability, conservatism and conformity.

Societies protect themselves from substantive change (and, therefore, from sociopolitical upheaval) through a complex dynamic of overt and covert sanctions against ideas and behaviours that deviate from the norms and interests prevailing at any given time. In 'democratic' and 'open' societies, these sanctions are largely informal, although more and more the liberal-democratic technocracies are tending increasingly towards a morass of regulation and legislation which further diminishes the possibility of authentic freedom in those matters that are fundamental to individual control over life and creativity. As this text is being finalized, a classic case study is unfolding, as the pharmaceutical industry teams up with the medical establishment to use legislation and regulatory regimes to remove from citizens in Europe and North America the free and accessible choice of naturopathic and homeopathic alternatives to pharma-medicine for maintaining and restoring health. This logic has gone so far in the case of the diagnosis of putative HIV 'infection' that intensely toxic pharmaceutical treatments, including AZT, are fast becoming mandatory by law throughout North America as a prophylaxis for asymptomatic people (that is, people who show no symptoms of illness), with HIV-positive pregnant women and infants – especially minority and poor women and their children – being the special target of such 'public health' regulations.[3]

It is on the area of informal sanctions that we must focus, however, because it is this phenomenon that is the real debilitating force, internalized as it is in our individual and collective consciousness. Regulatory and legislative structures and sanctions will be transformed only when the consciousness which spawns and authorizes them is transformed.

A critical element in informal sanctions is the fact that imbued in all of us is a socialized self-censorship facility which prevents us from exercising our capacity to see what *could* be, but is not yet, and prevents us from articulating, and often even from acknowledging, our depression and rage in the face of societal irrationality. We accede to, and share in, the irrational norms of thought and behaviour in the face of our fear of being seen as 'abnormal'. Behaviour that goes against societal irrationality is labelled 'antisocial', 'strident', 'radical', 'anarchistic', 'unbalanced', 'deviant' – indeed, 'insane'.[4]

Our need for material security, for acceptance, for tranquillity, for 'belonging', temper and subvert our need for authenticity and rationality. The person who asserts her vision and rationality against the irrational norm almost inevitably finds herself alone, and alone in a painful, almost unendurable way: an alien without the support of the group and without structures and norms to provide guidance, security and nurturance. Such alienation is pathological, just as the suppression of authentic self for identity within one's group is pathological. We are left with a painful dilemma, a double-bind: denial of self in order to maintain security of identity, and protection against alienation from the social grouping; or denial of social grouping for the existential integrity of self, and protection against alienation from personal value and vision. Both choices are alienating, pathological, anti-human, and 'death-dealing'. Neither choice can be tolerated in health.

This conflict, this tension, this implicit contradiction within our sociocultural relations, is a common threat to the health of each one of us, and is one of the roots of chronic ill-health in our societies. While this phenomenon is longstanding in society,[5] it is further complicated by developments in twentieth-century technological-industrial societies.

With the techno-scientific revolution that has made our earth so much smaller and our universe infinitely bigger, a transformation of human physical, psychological, intellectual, and spiritual-artistic relations within the environment is under way.

There are four developments which impinge quite directly on the matter of individual alienation. The first is the *rapid shrinking and dispersal of extended family groupings*, a phenomenon extensively documented within contemporary sociology. The village is dying, the family dissipated, the tribe erratically migrant. We are all lonely immigrants – in space, in time, in our minds – constantly required to establish new groupings, new identity, to accommodate new surroundings, new information, new ideas. More and more we are required to carry our 'territory' within our soul, without a permanent place or group into which we can project our significance and from which we can receive a concrete manifestation that *we really are here*. The implications of this development are profound, and it is certain that we are undergoing a transformation in the form and substance of human relating with human. And every individual has a personal stake because, at present, we have lost many structures that promoted health, and new relations must be created in their place.

A second development is the *communication explosion/implosion*. One aspect of individual life in a stable group setting was that the world did not change much – in fact, did not really exist outside the narrow experiential boundaries of the community. We now live with the world in our living-room. The information explosion has provided a source of vicarious experience which, in effect, puts the whole world in our hands, and hearts, and minds: we are becoming citizens of the world, perceiving and feeling direct effects of global events on ourselves.

There are many consequences. We are poorly prepared, intellectually or emotionally, to receive, accommodate and assimilate the vast amounts of information so haphazardly bombarding us. The result is sensory overload. The most dramatic consequence is a serious reduction in security, in significance, in comprehension, and in power – all critical elements in individual health. We cannot afford much loss in these areas, but the explosion of information and the implosion of our world are costing us dear. When we are daily bombarded with information – and misinformation – about world events, usually of a violent or catastrophic nature, and so complex that comprehension is virtually impossible, we lose our sense of personal control over our own lives, and hence our sense of security. Faced with teeming humanity struggling with the vagaries of natural and man-made catastrophe, we lose our sense of significance; individual significance pales as though we really were 'as flies to wanton gods' who 'kill us for their sport'.[6]

In identifying with *this* face of humanity – weeping, brutal, helpless, hopeless – we internalize it, and see ourselves in the mirror of humankind. The response, almost inevitably, is escape, isolation and inertia. We revert to whatever group, whatever activity, is safe, secure, insulated from the ugly face of the world, and which provides some nurturance of personal significance. We deny the vision that haunts our silent hours. We lose our sense of power.

A third development is a corollary to the communication revolution: the incredible *transformation of cultural processes*. Culture, which was once a gradual formative process bonding the various aspects of daily, individual, family and community life into a relatively comprehensible and coherent existence, is now a rapid, fragmented, remote and superficial process. Cultural integration has been lost to something akin to a spectator sport that represents the lowest common denominator of shared experience. This has devastating effects on established cultural patterns – most significantly that individuals and groups have neither control over, nor involvement in, their own cultural processes, and culture itself is increasingly reduced to a commodity.

Related to this is a fourth development: *non-creative structures*. Modern society is typified by non-creative structures in domestic life, in occupational life and in leisure life. When I speak of 'society', foremost in my mind, of course, is the specifically North American and industrialized milieu in which I live. However, the malaise and dilemmas I describe are applicable to all societies and every nation – with, of course, manifestations in some way unique to each situation – and especially in urbanized society, although anyone who has travelled extensively in rural areas in crisis has noted that such transformations are occurring rapidly there as well. The process of urbanization around the world has another face, called de-ruralization.

The stress is on convenience and expedience, on mass production and consumption, on fragmentation and modularization of production and work, on mass leisure activity based in passivity and spectatorship. We do not produce what we consume, nor consume what we produce. We do not own – even in a material, let alone in a spiritual-artistic sense – the product of our work. We do not take an active part in the source of our leisure; we have little control over our life-forces; our life-acts bear little relation to our authentic self; our activity is not an expression of self. We are components of production and consumption, replaceable and interchangeable, devoid of both ego-strength and involvement, and the nurturative feedback of identity. Individuality is obsolete and dysfunctional in a massified cycle of production and consumption of goods and services, most of which are non-essential and bear no relation to the authenticity of the people caught in the cycle.[7]

In this context, personhood is more and more a lost art in a system which is not structured to acknowledge 'persons', which is inherently 'anti-person', and in which we have increasingly lost the ability to bear witness to our own authentic personal being. We live non-creative lives immersed in non-creative structures. We are not possibilities in process, we are merely processed components in one perverse, ingrown possibility which feeds on itself.

Our health, then, is under constant threat, and this threat is accentuated by some of the recent developments described above. In fact, we are all, by definition, to varying degrees in a state of unhealth: lacking wholeness. And most of us are aware of this state; we know that we are not well. Why do we not do something about it? Why are the questions raised above – 'How do I act?' and 'Why do I not act?' – so very, very difficult? Part of the answer lies in ambiguity and risk.

Ambiguity

Our perceptions, and our motivation, are not simple. There are ambiguities in how we perceive the world, and in our needs and desires. And, as the original meaning of 'ambiguity' implies, we are continually 'driven in two ways'. This can be seen in what appear to be relatively insignificant dilemmas: we want to lose weight, but don't; we want to give up smoking, but don't. These insignificant dilemmas can be seen as moving on a continuum of dilemmas increasingly awesome in scope. We want to quit our job, but fear an uncertain future and the chance of failure. We want to be 'single again', but are unwilling to surrender love and security – the comfort and companionship of family. We want to help alleviate poverty, but want to establish our own comfort and security first. We want to be involved in the struggle for global justice, but ... there is not really very much we can do. It takes all our energy just to keep up; we can't seem to get involved.

Our personal dilemmas, whatever their scope, are not isolated. They are specific manifestations of a single personal phenomenon, a phenomenon which Rollo May describes as 'paralysis of will', which he defines as coming not specifically from the absolute absence or presence of power in our lives but from the contradiction or dissonance we experience at the intersection of our choices, a contradiction between our theoretical power to change a situation and the lack of power we experience in the very situations that we wish to change.[8]

Most of us live at the fulcrum of ambiguity. We live out conflicts, contradictions, dilemmas, dichotomies, facing a confusion of choices daily in a world that drives us in many directions. With knowledge and affluence comes ambiguity; with democracy comes ambiguity; with agnosticism comes ambiguity.

An ever-increasing proportion of people in modern industrial society 'know' more than ever before, and our knowledge expands daily. We are affluent in terms of both relative acquisition and choice. More and more we have the opportunity, and the time, for active involvement as citizens in the processes of society. At the same time we tend to an agnostic and sceptical position not only (not even *especially*) in a theological sense, but in a general sense, politically and socially – there is a growing hesitancy to accept authority and absolutes.

Directions are not clear. Reasons are not solid. And with the transformation of cultural process discussed above, and the related fragmentation of family and community, the experience of self is more and more remote from the increasingly disconnected sensations of social or cultural experience. We can no longer count on extrinsic factors to determine our choices and actions. We are not sure of anything, especially of what we want and what we should do.

A great deal of the nostalgia we often see among people who have experienced 'hard times' or crises – war, depression, external emergency – relates to the fact that, for a time, there was no ambiguity; one could live and act with single-minded dedication to a cause and to survival.[9] And I suspect that the recent phenomenon of the proliferation of cults, religious fundamentalism and mystic and psychic movements – let alone the conventional slavish adherence to the norms of corporatism, meritocracy and the consumer society – is a response to people's need to avoid ambiguity, to escape from freedom. We all seem to have a craving for the situation that allows no interpretation, no choice, in which we can act with absolute commitment not tempered by doubt.

The problem, of course, is that ambiguity is an essential element in freedom, a constant companion for the free person. In freedom there must be real, fundamental choice; with choice there will inevitably be ambiguity, of need and of thought. And the free person must learn to accept and deal with this ambiguity. Ambiguity is the creative tension that moves our possibilities. This element is central to John Ralston Saul's analysis of the effect of 'corporatism' on human consciousness: 'The corporate system depends on the citizen's desire for inner comfort. Equilibrium is dependent upon our recognition of reality, *which is the acceptance of permanent psychic discomfort.* And the acceptance of psychic discomfort *is the acceptance of consciousness'* (emphasis added).[10]

I have discussed health as a balance and harmony between and among needs, values and acts. The healthy person has integrated these elements. It is easiest for us to act when the action is directly related to a perceived immediate need consistent with our self-concept and in harmony with the norms of our group. Action becomes increasingly difficult when we are faced with choices that involve conflicts among these factors. In today's society, it is just such conflict which breeds the psychology of inertia. The key to learning to survive ambiguity lies in the concept of 'risk'.

Risk

Risk is the element of hazard in action. Risk is the factor of the unknown and the unknowable. There is an element of risk in every action we perform. The greater the potential benefit of the action, inevitably the greater will be the risk. Risk can usually be characterized by what can be gained or lost by an action. We are usually willing to risk an action in direct proportion with our calculation of the probability that the desired gain will be realized and no loss will occur. Most of us are willing to risk very little – we would rather maintain our status quo, no matter how unpleasant, than risk losing whatever little comfort is implicit in that situation. And we rationalize our inertia with 'common sense': the lesser of two evils, the devil we know versus the devil we don't know.

As a rule, this is a fool's game, for two reasons. First, in calculating risk we most often try to balance material tangibles against psychological intangibles. Rather than examining action in terms of health, we examine it in terms of security and comfort – which is only one aspect of health. We do this, of course, because it is easiest to identify the facets of material and physical security that might be exposed to hazard, and lost, through a certain course of action, such as quitting a job, going on strike, or changing a relationship. It is much more difficult to predict the intangible satisfaction: personal growth, or the material reward that might flow from that course of action. Second, and closely related, most calculation of risk is based in 'negative fantasy'. We fantasize the worst possible outcomes, and fear of these outcome, regardless of their probability, renders us powerless.

Growth is entirely dependent upon our willingness to risk. Risk is the process of growth. Human life without constant risk is morbid, degenerative, less-than-human. Risk is a venture into the unknown, to make it known. It is walking over the horizon to create new horizons. And risk has nothing to do with cost/benefit analysis. Even if loss and gain were relevant, we have absolutely no way of usefully analysing loss and gain before the fact. It is only our emphasis on security and comfort that introduces the loss-and-gain dichotomy.

Risk is a question of values, not acquisition. Every decision of risk is a choice of values. And it is directly related to the value we place on our self and our actualization, and on the value we place on our vision and the place of others in our vision. Risk is, therefore, a question of health. It is the decision to choose health by confronting the ambiguity of conflicting values. It is the decision to grow. Even while we may sometimes lose things we value when we take risks – that is why it is a risk – risk itself is rarely a losing proposition, because its consequences are growth and health and vitality. Choosing never to risk, by remaining inert, is *always* a losing proposition, because the consequences are stultification of self, unhealth, atrophy.

Ambiguity and risk are, simultaneously, threats to health and the very engines of health. They provide the creative tension for human growth, and the potential for human decay. Confronting this paradox is the perpetual challenge for the activist.

Notes

1. The most useful schema I know for conceptualizing the development of the healthy person is found in Abraham Maslow's 'psychology of being' and his classic construct describing a 'hierarchy of needs'. It is within this general framework that I formulate the perceptions which follow in this section. See Abraham Maslow, *Toward a Psychology of Being* (1968).

2. It is significant in this regard that most modern societies have largely ceased the direct curtailment of the freedom to act, resorting instead to a more subtle curtailment of vision through propaganda and morbid educational, cultural and political structures. The effect is the same – sociopolitical inertia – and is even more efficient in ensuring stability and popular passivity. For example, see Chomsky and Herman, *Manufacturing Consent* (1988).

3. The causes and effects of the 'premature consensus' on HIV and AIDS is a case study of its own, with an important and growing literature; recommended reading includes *Positively False: Exposing the Myths around HIV and AIDS* (Shenton, 1998); *Rethinking AIDS: The Tragic Cost of Premature Consensus* (Root-Bernstein, 1993); *Inventing the AIDS Virus* (Duesberg, 1996); *The AIDS War* (Lauritsen, 1993); *Aids and the Body Politic: Biomedicine and Sexual Difference* (Waldby, 1996); *AIDS and its Metaphors* (Sontag, 1989); and my own article, 'The Politics of AIDS' (*Third World Resurgence*, July 1994).

4. The practice, common throughout the world, of confining political prisoners in 'psychiatric hospitals', is one manifestation of this phenomenon. R.D. Laing's trenchant analysis of the politics of insanity in *The Politics of Experience* (1967) is provocative and valuable, as is the work of Michel Foucault.

5. Rollo May points out that this contradiction, or conflict, is age-old, a classic theme in human history, and that it will always exist as a potentially creative or destructive force in human affairs: 'there is no escape from living through this dialectical conflict of individual and society … no matter how much society is changed – and much of it cries to high heaven for change – there still will exist the fundamental dialectical situation of individuation against the conformist, leveling tendencies of the society.' *Power and Innocence* (1972), p. 229.

6. Michael Ignatieff uses the trials of King Lear to fascinating ends in *The Needs of Strangers* (1984), a very important treatise on social ethics and human reciprocity.

7. For profound, provocative and prophetic treatments of this theme, see Hannah Arendt, *The Human Condition* (1958); and Norbert Wiener, *The Human Use of Human Beings* (1954).

8. 'Thus, the crisis in will does not arise from either the presence or absence of power in the individual's world. It comes from the contradiction

between the two – the result of which is a paralysis of will.' *Love and Will* (1969), p. 187.

9. Rollo May provides an analysis of this phenomenon, using the specific example of wartime experiences. See ch. 8, 'Ecstasy and Violence', of *Power and Innocence*. Erich Fromm's *Escape from Freedom* (1941) provides a classic analysis of freedom, and the human tendency to submit to totalitarian structures rather than to exercise the responsibility of choice and the practice of freedom, in the face of awesome dilemmas. Jean-François Revel, in *The Totalitarian Temptation* (1976), explores the reasons why intellectuals are so prone to the Siren call of ideology in response to sociopolitical dilemmas.

10. See John Ralston Saul, *The Unconscious Civilization* (1995).

3

Confronting the Dilemmas: Beyond Inertia

True to the meaning of the rebel as one who renounces authority, he seeks primarily not the substitution of one political system for another. He may favour such political change, but it is not his chief goal. He rebels for the sake of a vision of life and society which he is convinced is critically important for himself and his fellows ... the rebel fights not only for the relief of his fellow men but also for his personal integrity. For him these are but two sides of the same coin ... he rebels against that system which permits slaves and masters.

Rollo May, *Power and Innocence*

How do we confront the dilemmas of action and integrity? How do we transcend the psychology of inertia? Strictly speaking, there are as many responses as there are individuals. Each human life is a new response to the contradictions of existence we have been exploring. This said, we can generalize and describe two generic responses which, on the surface, are in diametric contradiction to each other: *conformity* and *ideological radicalism*. In moving towards the formulation of our own response, it is useful to analyse the character and validity of these responses in the context of our previous discussion.

Conformity

This is the most usual response to the contradiction of values between self and society. We repress our sense of individuality, of authentic self. We adopt the established mode of behaviour and thought, based on extrinsic motivation and reinforcement. Nurturance and health come from identification with the group and its norms.

Action is reduced to reaction, essentially adaptation to the vagaries of socioeconomic hazard, cultural trends and techno-scientific change. Life becomes response to signals. The primary values are acceptance, security, stability and comfort.

Conformity is the easiest response to ambiguity and values conflict, because it follows the line of least resistance and is the response actively promoted by society. At the same time, it is an unhealthy response and carries with it intrinsic stress. This stress is usually relieved by *internalizing* the belief system that rationalizes the behaviour and attitudes adopted, by defining them as normal and natural. This belief system is inevitably ideological in character, and in most cases the fortress of ideology is supported by the buttresses of religion. The belief system is always implicitly or explicitly ethnocentric, and supported by the institutionalization of intolerance.

The response of conformity is the negation of the individual and of individual human potential, based as it is on the negation of the essential capacities and qualities that define human consciousness and creativity – remember the words of French critic and novelist Paul Bourget (1852–1935): 'One must live the way one thinks or end up thinking the way one has lived.'

Ideological Radicalism

Political revolution is often put forward as the antithesis of conformity, as *the* radical response. But in politics, as in physics, one revolution usually brings you back to your starting point; movement through 360 degrees leaves you standing still. Trading places with the slaver does not do away with slavery.

Political revolution (or its promotion) based on ideological doctrine is, ironically, fundamentally dependent upon conformity. Individuality and authenticity are again repressed. Extrinsic modes of behaviour and thought are adopted, this time based not on the prevailing sociopolitical structure but on a counter-doctrine, still extrinsic, dogmatic and absolute. This doctrine provides the necessary focus for motivation and reinforcement. Adherents are nurtured through commonality of cause and action with fellow doctrinaires. Action is programmed by the dictates of the ideology and its catechists, and activism is reduced to a militant response to the authority of doctrine. The primary value is dedication to the cause and to its code.

This response, once adopted, is relatively easy to follow, because the code is clear – all contradiction, all ambiguity, all doubt, is removed. Freedom of thought and act has been escaped, although the illusion of freedom remains. There is ego-gratification, in that harmony is established between belief and action; identity is provided through doctrinaire solidarity; sense of significance is strengthened by the role of the protagonist against the evil of society.

During the pre-revolutionary and revolutionary period, this response has its own perverse viability, and contains within it sustaining balance. Health is an individual phenomenon, and the ideologue solves the problem of health by recanting individuality – his own and that of others. In a very real sense the individual no longer exists; only the doctrine exists, and the individual is its tool – not as an entity, but as a function of doctrine (without exception, all existing formal ideologies, and religions, contain rigorous and explicit sanctions against individualism, personalism, 'selfishness' and non-conformity, in spite of incidental rhetoric to the contrary). Health, in the sense we have discussed it, is no longer a problem. This is tantamount to curing a headache by blowing out your brains.

In the post-revolutionary phase, there is no distinction between this response and that of conformity except, to some extent, for the small clique who are the leaders and who become the new regime. There is still, for the vast majority, repression, alienation, unhealth and conformity to an imposed ideology.

It is critical to explore the validity of the radical ideological response to societal irrationality and unhealth, because, for those of us who cannot or will not conform to prevailing 'truths', there is an almost irresistible tendency to establish (or adopt), and forcefully promote, countervailing 'truths'. We have been socialized to expect and to need order and identifiable, incontrovertible truth about reality and its workings. When we reject one truth, we feel the need to replace it with another. In this context H.L. Mencken observed:

The world always makes the assumption that the exposure of an error is identical with the discovery of the truth – that error and truth are simply opposite. They are nothing of the sort. What the world turns to, when it has been cured of one error, is usually simply another error, and maybe one worse than the first one.

This apparent need for order and truth blinds us to a more radical conclusion: it is not a particular false 'truth' that is the source of social evil; it is the notion of Truth itself. And it is not this or that invalid social dogma or doctrine that creates social injustice and dehumanization; it is dogma and doctrine in themselves that are contrary to justice, equality and the human possibility, and rob us of our freedom to think and act. To transcend inaction and dilemma, we need to transcend our need for order, truth, absolutes – that is, accept the inherent ambiguity of human existence.

The tendency towards the radical ideological response comes from the expectation of truth and absolutes, and from the corollary inclination to replace one system with another that is just as rigid, dogmatic and stultifying, based within the deeply rooted fatalism and inertia that characterize people who live under any long-established socioeconomic system and political regime.

It is largely a combination of these factors – an aversion to ambiguity, an expectation of absolutes, fatalism and inertia – that has led to the fact that virtually all great social movements have been initiated and given force by charismatic leaders. These are people of vision and action who were able to transfer their vision to – or articulate the repressed or inchoate vision of – 'the masses', motivating and mobilizing them to tremendous action. But such movements are ultimately limited in scope and potential, since they are based in one person's – or one small group's – power and ability to manipulate the consciousness and psychology of others. The force and direction of the transforming ideology are inevitably perverted to a force for conservatism and protection of a new political order, long before fundamental transformations in the social order are effected. Such movements are based not on authentic reflection, dialogue and action among individuals, but on de-individuation, on mass consciousness, on manipulation of persons as objects.

That such movements sometimes achieve some 'good' in terms of improving the base material human condition is more a statement about the incredibly oppressed state that has been the norm for human individuals throughout history than a statement about the value of charismatic leadership and ideological doctrine in social transformation. As long as the motivation for action is extrinsic, ideological and charismatic, such action will not lead to a more humane and sane world, because under such conditions the individuals in society are not the authors of their own consciousness and actions, and have neither authentic control over their own lives, nor authentic power in sociopolitical processes.

What is essential for positive social transformation is the development and expression of individual potential and vision in a milieu characterized by genuine personal freedom – which denotes both the possession of power and the absence of coercion and constraint – devoid of doctrine, dogma and sociopolitical absolutes. This leads to a third potential response to the dilemmas we have posed.

Humanist Radicalism

We are faced with complex dilemmas of social action, and with our own perceived powerlessness and inertia. We have a tendency to give way to conformism, but we know and feel that this is an unhealthy response. We struggle against conformism, and this leads us to the tendency to ideological radicalism (what Jean-François Revel called the 'totalitarian temptation') – it appears that the only tangible response to societal irrationality and institutionalized injustice is the forceful imposition of their antithesis, a new sociopolitical order. This meets our need for rebellion, a code and a cause. It provides an avenue for the expression of anger and pain, and antipathy to the prevailing social order. But our experience, reflection and analysis tell us that the ideological response is inadequate to the authentic capacities, qualities and potentialities of ourselves and others. The ideological response, once codified and set in motion, is a sociopolitical cul-de-sac, containing in itself all of the root social evils of the prevailing order.

Above, we discussed how ambiguity can be a positive state that drives our possibilities. Faced with the confusion and ambiguity caused by the fact that our commitment to growth and action is confounded by a lack of political certainty and the betrayal of ideological absolutes, we need a third option – an option that relies and builds on this ambiguity as a virtue and strength that drives and directs action and inquiry. I believe that *humanist radicalism*, as I shall describe it, provides the fertile ground in which such an option can develop. I borrow the term from Erich Fromm, and it will be useful to quote at length from his description:

What is meant by radicalism? What does *humanist* radicalism imply? By radicalism I do not refer primarily to a certain set of ideas, but rather to an attitude, to an 'approach', as it were. To begin with, this approach can be characterized by the motto: *de omnibus dubitandum*; everything must be doubted, particularly the ideological concepts which are virtually shared by everybody and have consequently assumed the role of indubitable commonsensical axioms.

To 'doubt' in this sense does not imply a psychological state of inability to arrive at decisions or convictions ... but the readiness and capacity for critical questioning of all assumptions and institutions which have become idols under the name of common sense, logic, and what is supposed to be 'natural'.[1]

Later in this essay, Fromm continues:

Radical doubt means to question; it does not necessarily mean to negate. It is easy to negate by simply positing the opposite of what exists; radical doubt is dialectical in as much as it comprehends the process of unfolding of opposites and aims at a new synthesis which negates and affirms.

Radical doubt is a process; a process of liberation from idolatrous thinking; a widening of awareness, of imaginative creative vision of our possibilities and options. The radical approach does not occur in a vacuum. It does not start from nothing, but it starts from the roots, and the root, as Marx once said, is man. But to say 'the root is man' is not meant in a positivistic, descriptive sense. When we speak of man we speak of him not as a thing but as a process; we speak of his potential for developing all his powers; those for greater intensity of being, greater harmony, greater love, greater awareness. We also speak of man with a potential to be corrupted, of his power to act being transformed into the passion for power over others, of his love of life degenerating into the passion to destroy life.[2]

Fromm completes his description of humanist radicalism:

Humanist radicalism is radical questioning guided by insight into the dynamics of man's nature; and by concern for man's growth and full unfolding ... humanist radicalism questions every idea and every institution from the standpoint of whether it helps or hinders man's capacity for greater aliveness and joy.[3]

Fromm's view of the appropriate stance and approach necessary to our historical dilemmas does not exist in isolation. There is a large body of description and analysis underlying the humanist radical response, including the central axis of feminist theory.[4] Nor do radical humanist social theorists provide identical analyses or conclusions, and there are often points of profound divergence. But we are not looking for *the* analysis, the one final and true description of reality; we are looking for an approach that offers the best available promise for human health and progress. Radical humanists *do* have in common an approach which begins with the root of 'humanness' and aims at fuller humanness; they also have in common a commitment to critical investigation, authentic consciousness, and radical intervention in reality in a rebellion against prevailing inhumanity, injustice and irrationality. They also share a realization that we seek not truth, but humanity; not structure, but community; not form, but creativity; not civility, but mutuality.

When we share this common base – what Fromm calls the 'core' – we can expect the contradictions of analysis and vision, and exult in them, and transcend them. Fromm characterized radical doubt as 'dialectical' because 'it comprehends the process of unfolding of opposites and aims at a new synthesis which negates and affirms'. When we share this common base we can participate in the creation of a new synthesis, sharing the responsibility for negation and the celebration of affirmation. It is the approach and its roots that are fundamental; the contradictions, the opposing views, are the perpetual ambiguities – the creative tension that powers human growth and progress.

How does the approach of humanist radicalism respond to the dilemmas of action and the psychology of inertia described above, which we experience ourselves and know is experienced by activists everywhere? The primary values in humanist radicalism are individual freedom, growth and health. Its one tenet is that freedom, growth and health for every human person are both possible and essential. Its ethic is that this individuality, characterized by these qualities, can flower only in a milieu of dialogue and mutuality.

The humanist radical approach is based on a profound distrust of absolutes and ideology, a distrust that contains the conviction that no idea or ideal is more important than a single human life. This does not mean that a person will not lay down her or his life for an idea, in the sense in which Eduardo Galeano (1983) quotes Salvador Allende: 'It's worthwhile to die for that without which it's not worthwhile to live.' It *does* mean, however, that we will not slaughter others in order to impose our own ideas, or visions.

Humanist radicalism recognizes the essential 'self'-centred quality of all action, and recognizes that the struggle for vision is the struggle for health. The humanist radical vision is a vision of and for self, but it includes all humanity. It considers as unacceptable the fact that some are free while others are slaves. It is based on the understanding that personal health is not remote from the health of others, and that it is only in sharing with others the perpetual struggle for freedom and growth and health that we remain free, continue to grow, and move towards fuller health.

Humanist radicalism is conspiracy. The word 'conspiracy' comes from Latin words that mean 'to breathe together', and combines the notion of mutuality of life with the image of hope. It is dedication to dialogue and mutuality, to shared vision, decision and action, because that is healthy and effective. To impose is to negate the human; to accept, dialogue, assert, accommodate, assimilate, share, is to actualize and affirm humanness. Humanist radicalism is open conspiracy: vision publicly professed, and asserted in action, a mutual celebration of human awareness, creativity, love and will, in a mutual endeavour to achieve the highest degree of integration of human faculties – emotional, physical, intellectual, and artistic – in creating new human feasibilities.

How do we move from dilemma, despair and inertia to active humanist radicalism? What is required of us is a personal affirmation. This affirmation does not deny nor exclude our dilemmas and our psychology; rather, it is an affirmation that is *transitional*, moving us from the state of despair and paralysis. And while it does not remove the sense of powerlessness, this affirmation makes powerlessness less oppressive and pervasive.

The personal affirmation required is an affirmation of self, and of vision: *I am so convinced that leaving social evolution to chance will lead to chaos, perpetuation of human misery, and the destruction of all things I consider remotely 'human', that I have no choice but to act personally on and with my society, regardless of my underlying fear that the essential transformations may never be achieved.* If, as human beings, we do not try, we may continue to live, but our humanness will wither and die. If we do try, we may fail, but at least it will be an individually and humanly meaningful failure; we will be striving for our own possibility; we will be 'in process', which is what humanness is. This affirmation makes the limits of personal power less relevant, by reducing our concern for ultimate effects and focusing on the need for self-affirmation and positive social action. Once I shift my perspective in this way, and make this affirmation, my tendency to despair no longer results in inertia, no longer saps my energy.

For this affirmation to be effective, we need to accept that *our* significance is not tied to what humankind eventually does, or becomes. Rather, our significance is bound up in what we, as unique individuals, do as 'possibilities in process' striving to actualize personal potential and the human possibility. Our significance is in the process of being and doing, of being whole and sharing our wholeness with others – a process that never ends. It is the practice of health, as discussed above.

This, of course, is not to say that the failures and successes that we create with others along the way are not important. They are extremely important, and intrinsic to our praxis – our ongoing learning and renewed action. But our significance is in the fact that we do act, rather than in the immediate results of our action. We will always be prone to despair, and inactivity, and impotence if we gain our identity and ego-strength from ends rather than means, from products rather than processes, from life after death rather than life through life, from acquisition rather than acquiring, from achieving rather than doing. We will be dead-in-life, unable to realize our personal human potential and essence.

The constant crisis of the activist is the danger of becoming 'burnt-out', of losing energy and the will to act. The activist is always seeking means to energize herself, to remain active. It is a problem of psychology, of motivation, of ego and identity. It is a problem of perception and a problem of health. We need to identify with a process, and gain our self-worth from who we are as agents, not from the products of our agency; from who we are as subjects, not from the objects we name. If we can maintain this perspective, we will be able to act, to 'risk a movement without being sure if movement would be better or worse in a hundred years or a thousand'.

The awareness and perceptions discussed here, if not prevalent, are of common enough occurrence that there is reason enough for hope, and hope enough for action. Our first step is not to decide whether our action will result in a new world but, rather, to decide, to affirm, that our consciousness must result in action whatever the eventual outcome.

When, as individuals, we see a glimmer of hope in this approach, feel the initial pulse of renewed energy, our attention needs immediately to turn to nurturance, to support, to dialogue – to assistance in keeping the hope alive and the energy in force. We need to find allies. At the risk of being simplistic, we must start talking to others. Within one mile of each of us at this moment there is at least one person who shares our concerns and perceptions and dilemmas; there are probably many more. We need to find him, her, them. And we need to share perceptions and visions, and analyse, and establish our personal constitution: 'I will act, because it is sane, and healthy, and human to do so. We will act together, because it is sane, and healthy, and human, and more effective to do so.' Then we can expand our group, working out ways to defeat the sense of personal futility, to test feasibilities, to transform the established irrationality.

This is how we can begin to develop an open conspiracy. We can conspire to transform our sociocultural reality, and we can proclaim our conspiracy to our society at large, professing our convictions that there are better ways, bearing witness to the potential of the human individual, asserting the fundamental need and right for every individual to practise freedom. We can publicly confront the established order with critiques of present practice and with alternative feasibilities. We can present and practise a conspiracy of women and men in free authorship of our own futures, openly, publicly, as a fact, a contradiction, in dynamic interaction with the established 'fact'.

Is there a reasonable hope that profound social transformation may ultimately emerge from such activism and 'conspiracy'? Part II of this book explores human beings and human society as open-ended 'possibilities in process', and provides an analysis of the essential qualities and capacities that embody our potential to transcend the conditions of our lives, and change the world.

Notes

1. From Fromm's 'introduction' to Ivan Illich, *Celebration of Awareness* (1970), pp. vii–viii.
2. Ibid., pp. viii–ix.
3. Ibid., p. ix.
4. See, for example, Carol Gilligan, *In a Different Voice* (1982); bell hooks, *Feminist Theory: From Margin to Center* (1984); and Jan Jindy Pettman,

Worlding Women: A Feminist International Politics (1996). For an excellent discussion of the contribution of feminist theory to the practice of science, see Hilary Rose, *Love, Power and Knowledge: Towards a Feminist Transformation of the Sciences* (1994).

Part II

Possibilities in Process

But we are free after all. We are bound not by the laws of our nature but by the ways we can imagine ourselves breaking out of those laws without doing violence to our essential being. We are free to transcend ourselves. If we have the imagination for it.

David Malouf, *An Imaginary Life*

4

The Missing Link

[Speech] was part of the development of a system of logical choice, of value judgement, and of projected symbol-making, through which new possibilities for reality could be consciously directed. This was a radical step of universal significance ... life *has* created the means for a conscious directing of potential and *we* are that means, aware of it or not, liking it or not.

Joseph C. Pearce, *The Crack in the Cosmic Egg*

I have argued that each of us – and all of us together – possesses the capacity to begin to transform ourselves, and the reality we share, and ultimately to contribute to bringing about a world of equality, justice and beauty. On what basis do I believe that we have the capacity to choose, as an act of will and as an act of humanity, to make this transformation? In this chapter I explore the essential qualities and capacities that embody our potential to transcend the conditions of our lives, and change the world.

Qualities and Capacities

First and foremost, human beings are creatures. By this I do not mean that humans were 'created' in the conventional sense; rather, we are beings whose existence has been, and remains, contingent on factors and processes external to ourselves. Moreover, our status as creatures is interconnected with the existences of all creatures: our being is one minute and integral part of a unified cosmic process of being.

Second, human beings are living creatures. We are a 'life-form'. This means that humans are capable of growth, movement, reproduction, and organic interaction with the other elements in our physical environment. While this observation may seem the commonplace of grade-school biology, it is best not to take it lightly, and I will come back to this point later.

Third, we are intelligent creatures. Conventional theory in biology presumes that each human, like all living creatures, possesses a comprehensive bank of information contained in the genetic map within the DNA molecule upon which, at least to some extent, our reflex behaviours and organismic capacities are based. However, humans transcend the limits of this genetic information base through cognition – the acquisition, through the nervous system and the mind, of extragenetic information and skills with which to interact reflectively with the environment.[1] Humans can learn. We can act in a non-reflexive manner on what we learn. We are not unique in this respect – the faculty of intelligence is widespread in higher earth life-forms. We are, however, unique in the quality and degree of our intelligence, which are closely tied to the facets discussed below.

Fourth, human beings are creatures who are self-aware. Humans are *conscious* creatures. We can perceive our world apart from ourselves, and ourselves apart from our world. We can 'objectify'. Humans may share rudimentary qualities of consciousness with other high-order mammals – for example, certain primates, whales, and dolphins. The extent to which human consciousness is more highly evolved is due to other effects of evolution – specialization of the nervous system and the limbs, the development of complex speech organs and highly complex symbolic language – and the subsequent creative extension of the human mind and body through technology and art. Not the least of the consequences of these developments is the exponential increase in our extragenetic information base, and the ability of each human individual to learn – through experience, and through communication technology, the arts and the sociocultural milieu – from the knowledge of humankind accumulated over millennia.

A fifth aspect of humankind is highly developed symbolic language. For our purposes, this development of symbolic language is unique, although the roots of our symbolic intelligence and language are shared by other creatures. It is always important to keep in perspective that we are a continuation of an evolutionary line and process, not an original and distinct event, and our present intelligent self acts with, not above, the reflexive mechanisms we share with other creatures.

A sixth aspect of humankind that leads to our potential to transcend the conditions of our lives, and change the world, is the capacity for abstraction. The capacity for abstraction is directly related to intelligence, consciousness and symbolic language – these being synergistic rather than linear developments. We are able to conceive mentally – Jacques Derrida's term 'conjure'[2] is provocative in this context – in spatial, temporal and intentional frames of reference. This is true for all humans, although the original development of human groups as more or less small and isolated cultural entities resulted inevitably in variations on this common theme, and some interesting diversity in ways of thinking and speaking about space and time, the abstract and the concrete. In general, however, people pattern reality within a spatial and temporal continuum – the present, in the context of past, becoming future. We abstractly impose form on reality by creating concepts, constructs and ideas. Direct manifestations of the capacity for abstraction are *rationality* and *imagination*.

Rationality, or 'reason', is the capacity to analyse the objective, visible world (deductively, inductively or intuitively) to reach conclusions and form systems of reality. Imagination is more complex and wondrous. Imagination creates in the mind what is not present or accessible to the senses. Imagination is the capacity mentally to create new ideas, or 'things', or states of things, or mentally to combine pre-existing ideas, things, or states in new forms.

A seventh aspect of humankind that promotes transformative action is the fact that we are 'emotional' beings, and we imbue objective phenomena with emotional content and value. While it is virtually impossible to describe emotion or 'feeling', we all know our emotional experiences of sadness, depression, love, hate, fear, elation. Emotion is our continuous, variable, psychosomatic response to the interaction between ourselves and the physical and social environment. I use the term 'psychosomatic' strictly, denoting the mind–body unity, the essentially organic unity which defines a human being. Emotion is our (only partially conscious) psychosomatic state, which is characterized by continually varying degrees and kinds of tension or satiation. And our emotional state is tied directly to values – the judgements we make or 'feel' about ourselves, our environment, and the interaction between ourselves and our environment. Our emotional experience is our most subjective experience.

Emotion, value judgement, and value projection are constants in the act of infusing the world with *meaning*, of making the world *personal*. The link between emotion and reason is intricate. Reason, in isolation, is extreme objectivity; emotion, in isolation, is extreme subjectivity. Reason and emotion never exist in isolation, do not form a dichotomy, and certainly are not antagonistic human qualities. Rather they are essential, harmonious functions of the psychosomatic entity, the human person – intricately interwoven manifestations of the subjective and objective fact of human consciousness.

The perception that emotion and reason are distinct, competing capacities, and the subsequent alternating cultural ascendancy of one over the other, springs from attempts finally to resolve the mystery of the relationship between humankind and our cosmos. This perception of an antagonistic dichotomy is one of the crucial misapprehensions and misapplications of human potential. In the reintegration of a functional unity of emotion and reason, of subjective and objective experience of reality, lie the seeds of a new, transformative activism.

All the preceding qualities and capacities lead to an eighth aspect of humankind that is central to the thesis of this book: we are able, to a large extent, to transcend our status in our environment. That is, on the basis of experience and learning, we can abstract in the present from the past to the future, and intentionally plan an act that changes ourselves or our environment, or both, and therefore alters our status in our environment. We can be the authors of our own individual and collective future. This is the unique promise of humankind. It is this capacity that sets us apart from other creatures, and it is only in the practice of this capacity that our status as humans is substantially different from that of other creatures.

Evolution is a dialectical and cybernetic process. With the power of our intellectual capacities we are able to experience and learn self-consciously within the feedback system of natural selection, life-processes, and the continuing interplay of health and pathology. We are able to assert ourselves purposely in this dialectic to alter the environment (social and natural) which acts on us to determine our status.

The ability to transcend the status of existence within an environment makes us creatures for whom freedom is a meaningful concept. The philosophical debate surrounding free will and determinism is age-old, and will continue as a central focusing theme of human introspection. Although the ultimate balance must tilt towards determinism in cosmic terms – 'time' is interminable; 'space' is unknowably vast; the variables are infinite – the principle of freedom of thought, will and action is not only valid, but essential.

To the extent that our environment, including our interminable biochemical and genetic past, acts on us, we and the material conditions in which we live, are determined. But we do have the freedom to resist 'fate' and transcend the conditions in which we find ourselves – especially since it is human beings, not Lear's 'wanton gods', who are responsible for much of the outrageous fortune which befalls us. In so far as we act on our environment – including our conscious selves and our societies – in a rational, humane and enlightened way to change the environmental agents that determine us, we are free, and radically so.

This perspective on 'determinism' is critical. The extent to which determinism is a factor in individual lives, or even in human epochs, is largely irrelevant. The universe is absolutely too large and complex to have definitive meaning or significance on any temporal or spatial scale relevant to human values, ethics or choices. What *is* critical is our potential for rational impact on the environment – impact based on acquired knowledge and wisdom, and the dialectic of human evolution. 'Determinism' is a red herring, a concept that has arisen as an answer to the wrong question – as is 'freedom' when it is discussed in this frame of reference, as the antithesis to determinism. Of course, we cannot absolutely determine the future. But this inability is a question of capacity and potential, *not* of freedom. This confusion has its roots in the tendency to formulate reality in terms of dichotomies of absolutes, and in the tendency to establish an absolute significance (or insignificance) for humankind – to 'call upon the universe to justify our existence', as W.H. Auden put it. The question of absolutes, whether of freedom or of fate, is irrelevant. What is relevant – and critically so – is that we are free to interact and transact within our environment, and the relationship is dynamic and complex. It is the exercise of this freedom to transcend and remake the human status that is our essential human possibility.

A ninth aspect of humankind, one that provides an awesome manifestation of our capacity to impact on and transcend environment, is that the human is a *technological* creature. We humans are able to create extensions of ourselves in the form of tools and machines that help us to choose and make our own future. Some of those tools, such as mathematics, language, music, are abstract. Others are extensions of the nervous system: telescopes, computers, radar, all the communications media. Others are extensions of the limbs: transportation and manufacturing devices, for example. Still others are replicas and modifications of natural phenomena: energy technology, and techno-chemical tools in such diverse fields as medicine or agriculture. The tools and machines of humankind are myriad and pervasive. What remains in question is the human capacity to use technology to enhance survival and the quality of life.[3]

A final aspect of humankind that conditions our capacity for transformative action is closely related to the technological aspect: the *artistic* character of human experience and creation. Just as technology is the extension of the human soma and rationality, so art is the extension of the human psyche, and the combined power of intellect and emotion.

Art is the expression of the emotional integration of perception, of aesthetic and moral values, of enduring beauty and knowledge. Art is the expression of human vision. Art personalizes life and reality, infusing existence with passion and significance. Art is the *avant-garde* of the human psyche, continually breaking ground on the frontiers of the possible, creating new modes of perception and human expression, reinterpreting the past, redefining the present, recreating the future before its time. The artistic character of humankind is the most mysterious of capacities: subjective, emotional, intuitive, unruly and brash, yet refined and penetrating; radically individual, yet profoundly universal. If our technology and our use of it tell us *what* we are, art tells us *who* we are, and could be.

Finally, to sum up the essential qualities and capacities discussed above that embody our potential to transcend the conditions of our lives and change the world: humans are cultural creatures, and the reality of humankind is a cultural reality. Culture is the collective response of the human group to its environment and its history. This response is multifaceted, manifested in sociopolitical structures; in collective norms and attitudes; in patterns of perception and interaction; in language, art, science and technology; in social and religious belief systems and corollary *mores* and relations; and in institutions such as the family, schools and civic associations. Culture is the collective ordering of the human environment on both the abstract and the concrete plane. At the same time, as cultures become 'set', a culture becomes, in a very real sense, human environment. What began as a creative response to environment becomes an environment itself. And, as environment, culture itself is a determining agent on the destiny of human individuals and groups.

The human being described in this chapter is an integral organism in the evolutionary event which is this planet Earth – itself a component in the larger cosmic event we label the Universe. Pierre Teilhard de Chardin's description of the human species as 'the axis and leading shoot of evolution'[4] is a theological assertion, not a scientific observation. Humans are not the axis of evolution. In fact, there is no axis of evolution – no linear, purposeful progression; merely (it is enough) infinite hazard and probability. This said, Teilhard de Chardin was at least poetically accurate in describing humankind as the 'leading shoot' of evolution – at least on Earth and near Earth. This status is not a result of cosmic design, but happenstance, in that the human is the one creature with the potential to take an active part in determining the course of its own evolution, and that of its planet. We have the potential to perform an intelligent, rational, creative role in the process of life development on the planet Earth.

And that is our starting point: we are intelligent, rational, self-aware creatures who, because of the tools evolution has provided, have some dynamic potential within the evolutionary process of which we are part. And this potential is essentially not only a possibility in a process but a possibility *in process*, itself ongoing and open-ended.

Place and Significance

I have elaborated this description of humankind on the basis of essential qualities and capacities, with little comment on the historical manifestation of these qualities and capacities, or their universal significance. Putting the human creature into cosmic perspective can be a shattering experience. We are one species of almost uncountable living creatures on a tiny planet of a remote galaxy in an infinitely vast, unknown space.

Someone once pointed out that a small coin held at arm's length blocks from our sight *a thousand galaxies* millions of light years away. In the context of this infinite vastness, it is not unlikely that the universe as known to humans contains a number of planets that support intelligent, self-aware, rational creatures, and that many of these life-forms are in a state of biological and cultural evolution considerably advanced beyond that conceived by Earthlings.

Even in our own world, humans are neophytes, having developed only a few hours ago in 'cosmic time'.[5] While we now ruthlessly dominate the planet, we will have to maintain ascendancy for millions of years to outlast our imperial predecessors, the dinosaurs. No doubt, the human creature is remarkable compared to the limitations of other known life-forms, especially when we try to infer the limits of human potential from the achievements accomplished in only the last few seconds of cosmic time. At the same time, with the present scale of misery and degradation on the planet, humankind is running the risk of pathetic failure – pathetic to the point of absurdity judged by the standard of apparent potential.

There may seem to be a contradiction here. On the one hand, an assertion of the cosmic insignificance and ludicrous imperfections of humankind; on the other, an analysis predicated on the premiss that there *is* significance to what we humans do with our possibility, as possibilities in process. How is this paradox resolved?

Humans are as insignificant as the most minute particle in the universe. Yet we share with that particle significance as part of the organic cosmic whole. Just as the cosmos is 'important' or 'significant', so are we. And to the same extent. In this sense, each human, and the human species itself, is of absolute cosmic significance. Not because we are different, or better, but because we are the same – an organism in a cosmic event and, in some ways, a microcosm of that event as it is happening here and now.

The source of human significance is intrinsic, not extrinsic, flowing not from uniqueness from the cosmos but from integral unity with the cosmos. In philosophical terms, human significance is ontological, not teleological. Our significance flows from the phenomenon of being, rather than from some abstracted, extrinsic end or design for being. Our significance lies in our status as possibilities in process and, therefore, in the degree to which our possibilities are optimized.

The essential factor in this possibility is the potential critically to direct the process itself.

An essential element of this question of significance is the concept of the individual. Human significance is the significance of the individual human, *not* the human species. The individual is the possibility in process; the species is secondary – not an end of evolution, but a vehicle. That is the evolutionary discontinuity which humankind represents. This is the central formulation which Chapter 5 will examine in depth.

Notes

1. See Carl Sagan's explanation in *The Dragons of Eden* (1977). This factor, and Sagan's discussion, will be discussed in greater depth in a later chapter. More recently, a fascinating and powerful new school of thought has developed that extends this notion of extragenetic learning to challenge quite fundamentally conventional assumptions about the extent of the role of the genes and DNA in the transmission of human learning; this theory turns reductionist science upside-down, and subordinates the role of genes to at most a technical component within a comprehensive field theory that sees human learning and collective 'memory' intrinsically integrated within an organic cosmic process, with the universe itself as an evolving, 'learning' organism. See Rupert Sheldrake, *The Presence of the Past* (1988, 1995); Ervin Laszlo, *The Creative Cosmos* (1993). Without positing an entire new visionary paradigm in the vein of Sheldrake, renowned Harvard-based geneticist R.C. Lewontin has led a more mainstream challenge to prevailing genetic theory in, for example, *The Genetic Basis of Evolutionary Change* (1974), (with S. Rose and L.J. Kamin) *Not in our Genes* (1984), and *Biology as Ideology* (1991).
2. See Jacques Derrida, *Specters of Marx* (1994).
3. There is a tremendous body of literature on this issue; see, for example, Norbert Wiener, *The Human Use of Human Beings* (1954); Hannah Arendt, *The Human Condition* (1958); Marshall McLuhan, *Understanding Media: The Extensions of Man* (1965); George Grant, *Technology and Empire* (1969); and Tom Darby, *Sojourns in the New World: Reflections on Technology* (1986).
4. In *The Phenomenon of Man* (1959), Foreword, p. 40.
5. For a delightful variation on the theme of cosmic events and evolution of life on Earth schematized in terms of human calendars, see Carl Sagan's explanation in *The Dragons of Eden*.

5

The Individual,
the Visionary

It is not Man who seeks a self, but each man.

Jacob Bronowski, *The Identity of Man*

Hitherto we have been discussing humankind in terms of essential characteristics and capacities. But the most essential characteristic is that each of us is unique in our manifestation of our humanness; and this uniqueness springs from the phenomena of consciousness and knowledge.

In any other species, the potential lies in the interaction between genetic base and environment. In a bee colony, one drone is indistinguishable from another – in form, function and behaviour. If the environment is maintained within the critical bounds necessary for a thriving colony, all patterns are predictable, deviance is rare, and the colony succeeds. If the environment is altered beyond critical bounds, the behaviour pattern will persist but will no longer be functional and useful, and the colony will be wiped out.

A conventional perception of humankind is that we are in essentially the same situation as the bee and other creatures – the difference being one of degree rather than kind. This view sees all humans as essentially the same: knowing the same things, thinking the same way, feeling the same emotions, motivated by the same base drives, acting out the same behaviours in reaction to the same stimuli. In fact, like snowflakes, no two humans are the same; and, since we are infinitely more complex than the snowflake, the individual differences among humans are also infinitely more complex. This is especially so in terms of potential for experience, thought, action and reaction.

The extent to which individuals behave in the same way – that is, the extent to which we *are* predictable – is largely the extent to which our society, its conventional wisdom and dogma, its mechanisms and institutions, deaden individual potential, and promote rote behaviours and perceptions. To this extent consciousness is stifled, thinking is stultified, experience is limited, individuality is negated.

The concept of 'the individual' is at the crux of all ideologies and theologies, the root of all social systems, the critical issue of virtually all battles. And well it should be. I want to examine the concept of the individual by discussing four essential qualities of individual being: consciousness, knowledge, motivation and action.

Consciousness

While humans inhabit a common physical universe, in another sense it is true to say that each person has, and is, a universe of our own, as a result of the quality of consciousness. We are aware of ourselves, distinct from our environment, our world. No quality defines us as individuals as this quality does. Consciousness is the key that unlocks the Pandora's box of all human qualities. Consciousness allows us to be subject of our own actions and perceptions rather than a mere object in a deterministic universe. Because of consciousness, we are aware of ourselves, distinct from others. We are able to objectify – that is, we see objects apart from ourselves upon which, or with which, we can act; or which can act on or with us. As individuals, we are not only *in* our world, but can see ourselves as part of our world, acting on and *with* it.

Consciousness is a threshold which, once crossed, opens up a universe for humans: language, objectivity, knowledge, curiosity, creative learning, subjective action, intrinsic motivation, hope, intention, choice – that is, a universe in which we have an active role in evolution.

And this active role is individual. This is the radical transformation that flows from consciousness: awareness of self, and therefore the ability to act on oneself and one's environment – as a matter of individual thought, individual choice and individual will. Our relationship with our world is essentially an I–Thou relationship.[1] The starting point of all human action is 'I', as perceived apart from but related to you, he, she, it, we and they.

Human beings are autonomous creatures. Our species is defined by transcendence of species-dependence. We are not a function of our species. We are not components. We are complete in ourselves. The group is our tool – the very *first* tool. In other creatures, the needs of the group supersede those of the individual; humans, on the contrary, create groups to meet individual needs. Rather than the individual being a function of the group, for humans the group is a function of the individual. In fact, survival of human society is dependent on the individual.

In nature, evolution proceeds by genetic mutation and natural selection, through survival of the most successful mutants. Mutation is an *individual* event, not a species, or societal, event. This is true of even the lowest of life-forms. With humankind the process is taken even one more step: the evolution of which each human is part is now *extragenetic* because of consciousness. It is based not only in individual genes but in individual experience, knowledge, wisdom, choice and action, which can change the individual and his or her situation.

This is the evolutionary progression of which humankind is the present furthest extension. What humanity ultimately accomplishes with this extragenetic potential as an agent of evolution remains to be seen. But each individual's potential is to be the 'missing link' between him- or herself and a more complex form of conscious, creative life. The human individual represents a significant development in an evolutionary progression, and *could* be the link to another even more remarkable phase.

This is the essence of the human capacity. As a norm, however, the present status of human development does not reflect this capacity. Only rarely does our *capacity* become *capability*, because consciousness is deadened and society pre-empts the development and expression of individual potential. The tremendous capacity for autonomy and creative life within human society has not even begun to be realized. But it could be, and might, for the threshold of consciousness has been passed. It only remains for critical consciousness to be valued, developed and expressed as a universal social norm.

I recognize that this emphasis on the free individual as the preeminent unit and basis of society is a controversial assertion that is challenged by those communalists of all stripes – cultural, religious, nationalist and ideological, and from both the Left and the Right –

who insist that humanist individualism is a perversion of natural laws and human nature, and a danger to society and the nation. Some will even insist that this notion is culturally imperialist, or *bourgeois*, a subversive idea from the decadent West. This is nonsense. Humanism is neither a Western nor a modern idea; on the contrary, it is universal and as old as human thought, and has constantly been repressed as a threat to the prevailing order. I can only respond that the argument of such cultural relativists and ideologues is not merely with me but, far more importantly, with the thousands and millions of people in their own societies, and internationally, who demand freedom from the repression that religious, political and cultural elites impose on all who would dare to resist the hypocrisy and deceit of their hegemony, and attempt courageously to think and dream and live free in a future of their own creation.

Knowledge and Truth

Knowledge is possible because we have consciousness; that is, because we *are* conscious – aware of ourselves as distinct from anything 'out there'. Knowledge is an objectification of relationships. It is the conclusion we reach about a thing or a state of things, *as it relates to ourselves*, the 'knowers'. While knowledge is an objectification – that is, the perception of a thing as an object distinct from self – to have meaning and significance knowledge is also the perception of the *relationship between* a thing and oneself.

Knowledge is simultaneously both objective and subjective. Its essence is *relative* and *subjective*. Knowledge is a strictly individual phenomenon – it is not in books, but in individual minds. Knowledge is the fruit of experience, and experience is the sensation of the individual. Because we are conscious, we experience. We interact with our environment and perceive ourselves doing so. We perceive our environment, relationships within our environment, and relationships between our environment and ourselves. We organize our realities, pattern our realities, draw conclusions about our realities. These conclusions are our knowledge.

But the individual experience is an internal happening – perception and experience happen internally, in the mind. The experience of burning a finger happens not at the tip of the finger, but at some remote electrochemical locus of the brain. Experience is a function of *awareness*, not external reality. The anaesthetized patient does not experience the scalpel; the dead do not grieve.

This is not to say that there is no external concrete reality. But we do not experience external reality directly; rather, we experience the sensations that are manifested by the interaction between our nervous system and external reality. Our nervous system, of which the brain is the dominant component, mediates the interaction between each individual and her environment. What happens to (in) us is a function of mind, not of external factors. Experience is strictly individual; as is perception; as is knowledge.

When two people share a common external situation, they do not share a common experience. In a very real sense there are two situations: one situation is that of person A, and the other of person B. Person A's situation includes person B; person B's situation includes person A. The manifest characteristics of the two experiences may be sufficiently similar for the two individuals to feel a shared bond when they reflect upon what has happened – but more than they will ever realize, the two experiences were unique.

Examples of this can be seen in reactions to 'art'. For example, two people might go to a film or play. The reaction of one person might be 'That was fine!', but the other reacts: 'It was trite, boring.' The same type of thing is seen in the variety of reactions to music, or to poetry – to all the art media. A more complex example is seen in the contrary reactions of two people observing an anti-government demonstration: one sees democracy in action against the villains of the decadent establishment; the other sees a threat to the stability, order, and national loyalty which are the keystones of his own concepts of democracy. Steve Biko's experience of Soweto was different from John Vorster's.

Experience, perception and knowledge are unique and individual. The extent to which they can be shared is a tribute to self-awareness and our ability to communicate. That fund of knowledge that is accepted as common among a group of people has been arrived at through a negotiation of individual perceptions and a common agreement that the sum of individual experience leads the group to a common conclusion about reality.

But the commonality of *understanding* about a unit of knowledge is extremely variable, and dependent upon the directness and scope of the experiences that caused us to accept this as knowledge in the first place. Even when a codified unit of knowledge ('What goes up must come down'; 'Columbus discovered America'; 'All persons are born equal'; 'e = mc²'; 'War is hell'; 'Eleven million people were exterminated by the Nazis') is mutually agreed upon, our understanding of its meaning, and the significance of its meaning, remain very individual. And, of course, understanding and significance are the core of knowledge.

In *Dragons of Eden*, Carl Sagan very valuably shed some light on the nature of human intelligence, and came to critical conclusions about individuality. Sagan distinguished between two generic types of knowledge: genetic knowledge – information transmitted in the genes; and extragenetic knowledge – information created through experience (direct or vicarious). Basic life-forms rely virtually entirely on genetic knowledge. The more complex the nervous system of the life-form, the greater the role of extragenetic knowledge, hence the greater the 'individuality' of the creature.

Humankind represents a near-quantum leap in the primacy of extragenetic knowledge – we are the creature whose being is predicated upon extragenetic learning/knowledge, and whose existence and survival depend upon it. The key factors in this regard are, first, consciousness; and second, the immense complexity of the brain and nervous system, allowing virtually uncountable possibilities in terms of bits of information and the dynamics among bits of information. As Sagan points out, the implications of this phenomenon for the sanctity of the individual are pivotal:

If each human brain had only one synapse – corresponding to a monumental stupidity – we would be capable of only two mental states. If we had two synapses, then $2^2 = 4$ states; three synapses, then $2^3 = 8$ states, and, in general, for N synapses, 2^n states. But the human brain is characterized by some 10^{13} synapses. Thus the number of different states of a human brain is 2 raised to this power – i.e. multiplied by itself ten trillion times. This is an unimaginably large number, far greater, for example, than the total number of elementary particles (electrons and protons) in the entire universe, which is much less than 2 raised to the power of 10^{13}. It is because of this immense number of functionally different configurations of the human brain that no two humans, even identical twins raised together, can ever be really very much alike. These enormous numbers may also explain something of the unpredictability of human behaviour and those moments when we surprise even ourselves by what we do. Indeed, in the face of these numbers, the wonder is that there are any regularities at all in human behaviour. The answer must be that all possible brain states are by no means occupied; there must be an enormous number of mental configurations that have never been entered or even glimpsed by any human being in the history of mankind. From this perspective, each human being is truly rare and different and the sanctity of individual human lives is a plausible ethical consequence.[2]

Before moving on, a clarification is in order with regard to our assumptions about objectivity, about knowledge, about 'truth'. I stated above that knowledge is essentially subjective and relative – personal – because our experience, hence our perceptions, are subjective and self-centred, that is, related to ourselves. The human mind is not capable of purely objective cognition, a reality which is an essential element of the formulation of the Principle of Indeterminacy, and the 'observer effect' in physics, and in the mathematics of Gödel, Turing, Church and Tarski dealing with the 'problem of decision'.[3]

Beyond the mere fact of our subjective stance in relation to reality, human knowledge is also constrained by the limitations of the organizing principles of our perceptual apparatus – our senses and the nervous system:

> we are in any case mistaken if we think of our picture of the world as a passive record.... It is the implication and the expression, in symbolic form, of all our dealings with nature. The picture is not the look of the world but our way of looking at it: not how the world looks, but how we construct it.[4]

Because we can know only in so far as our perceptual apparatus can perceive, and as we relate what we perceive to ourselves, absolute knowledge is not a human possibility. This conclusion, while fairly obvious and certainly accepted by those who search on the frontiers of knowledge, is in many ways a heresy against the human self-image. We act. We act on the basis of what we know. We defend our actions with knowledge. In so doing, we pretend that what we know is absolute. Thus comes 'Truth'.

The introduction of the concept of truth into the human collective consciousness tells us not so much about knowledge as it does about the human need to know. As a construct, truth has no validity and is essentially destructive to human efforts to order reality meaningfully. In any even tentative, operational sense, the concept of truth can be only an abstract *quality*: an objective and absolute correlation between external reality and what humans 'know'. In this sense, truth is still an ideal, but within the realm of the possible, because it is *possible* that some of the beliefs held to be fact within the human fund of knowledge may actually correspond accurately to objective reality. But we can *never know* whether what we hold to be knowable fact is, in reality, true.

Truth should not be the goal of human endeavour, nor should the presumption of truth be the rationale of human choice and action. Only 'knowledge' – defined as an ever-widening, ever-changing understanding of reality – is possible. Knowledge in this sense should be our goal, and our rationale. And a deep appreciation of the limited, ever-changing character of knowledge should guide our every step.

This is not analytic or positivistic quibbling. How we think about truth and knowledge is important because it determines how we act. It determines the process of our thoughts, and the process of our behaviour. Truth and knowledge have become synonymous. This blinds us to a critical reality – a limitation – of our existence. And we need to be aware of our realities, our limitations, if we are to transcend them, and of our capacities if they are to be realized.

Truth is merely a unit of commonly accepted and practised knowledge which has become non-negotiable because of its role in justifying human actions or social structures. It is denial of the essential individual and subjective nature of consciousness, experience, perception and knowledge. Truth is a denial of individuality; it is a denial of the capacity and potential of human individuals to be autonomous in thought and act. Truth is a denial of the intrinsic potential of individuals to develop and grow as the authors of their own being and universe.

The potential of humans is typified by doubt, and question – not by certainty. Susan Sontag once declared that the best answers merely 'destroy the question' and lead to more questions. Doubt has led humankind on the quest for understanding and the development of potential. And this quest directs human evolution. Truth kills doubt, halts the quest, and stops evolution. The death of doubt would be the death of humankind as an evolving species.

Ants, bees and cockroaches do not doubt. Nor do the zealots of creed or ideology who terrorize and try to obliterate whatever creative human spark threatens their personal version of truth. These guardians of Truth have repressed and slaughtered humankind for millennia. And those individuals who have most dramatically resisted this repression and fomented substantive change have begun by doubting, by questioning, by challenging and eventually confronting the established conventional truths.

This tradition of resistance against tyranny, whether it is based in race, or gender, or class, or religion – indeed, it is usually based on all of these equally – continues today. We have seen it in the struggle for freedom and democracy in South Africa, in Burma, in Indonesia and East Timor; in China, in Guatemala and El Salvador and Colombia and Peru; we see it in Palestine and in the remarkably courageous (and underreported) anti-Zionist peace movement in Israel; we see it in the resurgent organizing among the working poor, marginalized minorities, and progressive intellectuals in the industrial-ized and newly industrialized nations – in Latin America and Asia as well as Europe and North America; we see it in the untiring efforts of feminists worldwide to challenge patriarchy and militarism and forge a new politics that is radically informed by the diverse voices, experiences and values of women; we see it in the resistance among radical Catholics to the reactionary politics and autocracy of the Vatican, and among secular Muslims to the theocracies that repress millions in the name of a false Islam.

All this is a legacy and continuation of the creative courage of countless people over epochs – some famous, but most anonymous to history – who have embraced radical doubt and resisted oppres-sion and tyranny. Like them, each of us is capable of conquering our dependence on truth and developing a reliance on the exhilaration of new knowledge and increasing understanding, and using this knowledge to contribute in our own way to changing the world. This is within our power, and corresponds to our realities.

Motivation

From consciousness, experience, perception and knowledge come the individual's world-view and self-concept. And from these comes motivation – the movement to action.

As the individual develops, she evolves a functional overview of self, the world, and the relationship between them. It is a pattern of perception about how 'things' work, and how to affect 'things'; it is conclusions about how 'things' are, how they could be, how they should be, and conclusions about one's self in this continuum. This overview is cumulative, dynamic, ever-developing, and it is the fruit of experience. It is uniquely individual – there has never been a self quite like this before; there has never been a self-concept and world-view quite like this before; there never will be again.

From our self-concept/world-view flows the individual motivation to act – to maintain or to develop (change) the way things are; to maintain or to develop (change) self as self-perceived. The primary drive of human individuals is not survival of the species, is not survival of the group, is not even survival of the physical self. Rather, our primary drive is the survival and development of the personal self as reflected in self-concept and world-view, and this drive includes, of necessity, the survival and development of our world as we perceive it must be for us to interact in an integral manner consistent with our self-concept.

The human individual is a visionary whose primary drive is to live his or her vision. Our reality is in the realm of vision; our action is in the realm of realizing or maintaining our vision. And all these are inescapably individual in essence. Our individual vision is all we know. It is our being, and our reason to be. Each person knows she is an individual, knows there is really nothing meaningful except awareness of self and vision of the world. It is inevitable that our primary drive is to maintain the integrity of this vision. Our vision is our self, and survival of the self is dependent upon the survival of the vision. If the vision is threatened, the physical self is irrelevant, valueless, and risking physical well-being is a small cost to protect the vision.

Those for whom physical survival and well-being are the vision are driven to stay alive and will do anything to maintain life. Those for whom the quality and *state* of life is a vision are driven to maintain or achieve that state and that quality, and will die to do so.[5] In human history the latter is the more common. The course of human history has been driven by individual and collective visions of a better world, and the ongoing struggle to turn vision into reality.

The notion that the basic human drive is that of animal survival is myopic. It is a manifestation of the legacy of perverse, death-dealing ideologies and theologies that have perpetuated the status of most human existence at base, subhuman levels throughout history. The implications of individual autonomy and vision are so resounding and threatening to those whose vision is immersed in and dependent upon the status quo that no nurturance, no tolerance, can be allowed for individuality, for autonomy, for free will, for creative free expression of self. But humans, everywhere, continue to maintain and express self. We do author autonomous, individual actions. This is our potential, our disposition, and our will.

Action

Human acts are individual vision and will, transferred to concrete reality. Human beings act with conscious intention. We create action purposefully, wilfully, to achieve effects. Our ability to act flows directly from the continuum of consciousness, experience, perception, knowledge, vision, motivation. Our individual actions are authored creatively – reflectively rather than reflexively – as direct expressions of self. The actions of humans are statements of individuality. Our acts are the proof of our individual essence. The human is the creature for whom 'individuality' is the essential ontological manifestation.

The Individual in Society

Given this individuality, what of society? What of the species? The evolutionary advance that is 'humankind' is the transcendence of fatal species-dependency, and the corollary potential for individually authored evolution. We can, to a significant degree, direct the evolution of our species. And, as has been shown, the direction for human evolution is provided by the knowledge, vision and actions of individuals.

One of the first evolutionary acts of humankind was the creation of communities and societies in which individuals took (and take) part for their own survival. It was for the success of individuals that societies were (and are) formed. The success of individual human beings depends on successful interaction within our human environment as well as – probably more than – other aspects of the 'natural' environment.

It is essential that individuals negotiate to arrive at mutually acceptable actions on reality. Beyond this, it is obviously of mutual benefit for individuals to share their actions for more effective impact on reality; as a result, we have co-operation, group action and, therefore, society. For this to be possible, it is necessary not only for each individual to create his or her own world, but for individuals to share with each other in a mutual creation which meets the needs of each individual and all individuals as a collectivity. This necessitates not only dialogue, but an ongoing negotiation among perceptions of reality and motivations for action to arrive at perceptions and actions that are mutually acceptable *and* meet individual needs. Individual needs, however, remain the prime consideration and prime mover. In this sense societal aims are *individual* aims, established within a collectivity of individuals.

So, on one level, for reasons of pragmatic self-interest, individuals author their group. But the motivation goes well beyond this profane selfishness (although selfish it remains – it can be nothing else): our sense of self makes it virtually imperative that we share our creative existence with others.

We saw earlier that the awareness of our uniqueness creates a countervailing need for 'identity', for relatedness, for sameness. 'Identity' (from the Latin *idem*, meaning 'same') refers to that quality of humans by which we relate to creatures or things outside ourselves in terms of their essential sameness to ourselves. Our awareness of identity with our environment balances our sense of essential 'aloneness', and provides a sense of significance to our individual existence.

Ego (I-ness) and Identity (same-ness) provide the balancing poles of our individual self-concept, from the awareness of which flow all our interactions with the environment. This is the key to understanding individuals in groups. I without thou is meaningless. As discussed in Chapter 2, I gain my meaning and significance from linking my personal ego with my identity with my fellow humans; my relations with other people constitute an I–thou dialectic, and so must be my creation of the world if the intrinsic balance of my Self is to be maintained and nurtured.

To subordinate my identity needs to my own expression of ego is unbalanced and pathological; to subordinate my ego-expression to my identity needs is unbalanced and pathological. We are always striving for balance and harmony between expression of ego and identity; in fact, it is in the striving for such harmony that the human journey unfolds. The harmony lies not in *balancing* a dichotomy, but in doing away with the dichotomy in a situation in which our expression of self, and our expression of self-in-group, are a unity intrinsic in all acts. And such unity does not diminish our significance; it *is* our significance. The human is the individual with the potential for creative harmony within the society she creates. If this is the human potential, what of historic reality?

We have a tendency to see the individual and society as a dichotomy in which a choice must be made: *either* the individual, *or* society – as though 'society' was an entity apart from the individuals who comprise it. Given history, and the tension between our ego and identity needs, this is not at all surprising. Ultimately, however, there can be no dichotomy. To function successfully, individuals and society must be a unity. A society in which one subordinates or negates the other is a malfunctioning organism. Societies that distinguish between the aims of individuals and the aims of society have lost their vitality and validity as societies.[6]

There are two particularly destructive versions of this tendency. The most obvious is totalitarianism, in which society has been totally incorporated with the identity and structures of the state, as entity, and all individuality is totally subordinate to statism. Less obvious, but equally dangerous in the long run, is the utilitarian model in which society has been transformed into a tyranny of the plurality, where individuals are subordinate to an awesome process of power-brokering among pressure groups and factions hidden behind a parliamentary façade and the rhetoric of 'national interest'. This is usually called democracy, although it is more correctly called 'corporatism', as analysed by John Ralston Saul and others.

The aims of society – 'state' is *not* synonymous with 'society' – ought to be the articulated, collective aims of the individuals who are the society. Humans derive their significance not from the success of a state or a nation but from their success as individuals in dialogue, and in mutuality of existence, expressed through and with their society. The human individual is an entity; society is a relationship among entities; the state should be a *function* of a society, established and moved by individuals, with none of the qualities or capacities of an entity.

When a state becomes an entity in the minds of its citizens – which is the history of states – individuals are subordinated to its existence and removed from the possibility of authentic expression of self. The aims of the state become the aims of individuals; this is an inversion of human potential, and antithetical to human actualization. The state takes on its own being, deadening authentic individual consciousness and replacing it with a blind assumption that the status quo must be, because it is, and that humans are fatally immersed in the predetermined status quo.

Statism, corporatism, ethnocentrism, racism, massification, domestication, conformism, reflexive behaviour, appear to be norms of human 'societies'. How can this apparent reality be reconciled with the more vibrant vision of humankind proposed here?

Totally reflexive behaviour is not the condition of humankind – the richness of human behaviour even under the most squalid and horrific of circumstances is awesome. The extent to which we human beings do not achieve our potential to be the creative authors of our own vision is due to a tremendous set of socialized perceptions – Truths – which promote a limited consciousness and prevent the development of critical awareness of our human essence and potential. We lack critical awareness of the natural phenomenon of which we are an integral part, and of the dynamic, dialectic interaction which defines our relationship to our environment. Many of our truths function, ultimately, to prevent our self-actualization, as individual and in groups.

Chapter 6 examines some of the more damaging aspects of conventional perceptions and consciousness which inhibit the potential of human individuals and society.

Notes

1. See Martin Buber's classic elaboration in *I and Thou* (1970).
2. Carl Sagan, *The Dragons of Eden* (1977), p. 42.
3. See discussion on the problem of decision and its significance in Jacob Bronowski, *The Identity of Man* (1965), in the added supplement on 'The Logic of Mind'.
4. Bronowski, *The Identity of Man*, p. 35, emphasis added.
5. Martin Carter, poet and activist from Guyana, said: 'we who want true poems must all be born again, and die to do so' (1961).
6. This dilemma is exposed eloquently by John Ralston Saul, most recently in the Massey Lectures sponsored by the Canadian Broadcasting Corporation, published as *The Unconscious Civilization* (1995).

6

Challenging the
Established Rationality

> Critical thought strives to define the irrational character of the
> established rationality (which becomes increasingly obvious) and to
> define the tendencies which cause this rationality to generate its own
> transformation.
>
> Herbert Marcuse, *One-Dimensional Man*

Significance is a person's sense of self. It has no objective reality
except in our personal 'vision'. Humankind has no destiny. We were
not created for a purpose. We have no end, and are the means to
no end. We share with all existence the status of one of the infinite
possibilities in the process of existence. We have no significance
beyond this – it is enough, and all.

This said, rather than being fatally destined to be passive victims
of these inexorable processes, one of our possibilities is to work to
transform ourselves and act to change the world. It is our capacity,
each of us, to become constantly and critically aware of self as a
possibility, and to assert our consciousness and rationality so that we
are active and creative participants in the complex processes of which
we are part, constantly remaking ourselves and the world in our daily
actions with others.

This is our possibility. But common perceptions about reality
interfere with this possibility and prevent us from acting as full and
authentic agents of our own process of being. This chapter attempts
to 'define the irrational character of the established rationality' by
challenging several central assumptions on which this established
rationality is built:

- Humans exist in definite dimensions of time and space.
- The universe operates on a rule of linear contingency – cause and effect.
- The universe was created for a purpose.
- The human is the keystone of that purpose, and its ultimate creature.
- Humankind is master, by intent of creation, of all other existence.
- Humans have a 'nature', static and immutable.
- Humans are subject to immutable natural and moral laws.
- Human destiny is predetermined.
- History is linear.

These perceptions are shared, in one form or another, by the vast majority of us, and undermine our efforts to adapt to and change our environment. Even those of us who assume that we have freed ourselves from these perceptions still often think and behave as though they were valid and true. Science and politics themselves are practised largely within the pragmatic parameters of this mechanistic paradigm, regardless of formal rhetoric to the contrary. Therefore it is essential to scrutinize and test our commitment to these assumptions, and even our ultimate capacity to escape them, rational or not. I will scrutinize each of them in turn.

Humans exist in definite dimensions of time and space

We perceive ourselves in 'time' and 'space', but time and space are essentially functions of perception itself. They are constructs which allow us to organize experience meaningfully. We create our perceptions of events as progressive action within a prescribed space. Yet we know, intellectually, that time and space have no absolute existence outside our minds. For time to exist it must have a demonstrable beginning and end; for space to exist it must have demonstrable boundaries. Neither of these conditions exists except as an abstract human hypothesis.[1]

As a functional construct, humankind has created a 'universe' – all existing space – the boundaries of which are known not by observation but by definition, 'the outside limits of what is'. In cognitive terms it might be said that it is the 'idea' of infinity – no limits on what is – that creates the limits that we call space and time. We can abstractly conceptualize infinity, the condition of there being *no* limits on what is. In practical perceptual or experiential terms, however, infinity cannot be conceived as anything but an abstract negation of our perception of boundaries. The organizing principles of the mind and senses set boundaries, imposing spatiality on our perceptions of reality.

Similarly, we have designated the beginning of the universe (space and matter) as the 'beginning' of time, before which time was not. Time is our concept of 'duration' – the period during which things have existed in finite space. It is another boundary on what is. Time, like space, has its antithesis, conceived but not perceived, called 'infinity'. Time, as perceived by the human mind, is essentially spatial in its conception: duration of movement measured in spatial terms. A watch measures time on the basis of the movement of a hand through a given space. Our temporal terminology and measurement are arbitrarily correlated to the duration of movement through, or action in, space.

Discoveries in physics since the beginning of the twentieth century have altered the meaning and significance of time and space for the theoretical scientist, and these discoveries are slowly filtering down into applied science and the conscious perceptions of ordinary people. So even as an artificial construct, time is not absolute by definition. As scientific and technological advances narrow the gap between our perceptions and our scientific knowledge, our perceptions of time and space are being modified: space, as a functional construct, is altered by the time required to traverse its area; distance is altered by its character as a separating agent; time is altered by the duration (and number) of events that can be accomplished within certain temporal limits; 'duration' takes on new meaning as a construct which not only unifies space and time in the abstract but also represents a relationship which can be observed and which seems to be defined by 'laws'. These (ephemeral) laws can be used by science to delve deeper into the natural reality behind our concepts of time and space.

The universe operates on a rule of linear contingency – cause and effect

Spatiality and temporality are profound determining agents on perception and consciousness. We presume the reality of space and time, and from this presumption flow other perceptual sets of a seriously inhibiting nature.

One such 'set' is that of cause and effect: every event has a cause;

these causes can be discovered and explained. This set inhibits the extent to which we appreciate the critical limitations on both our perceptions and our knowledge, and conditions the tacit, but pervasive, belief (1) that there are events; (2) that all events have discrete causes; and (3) that these discrete causes can be identified. These are false and, more importantly, limiting perceptions. There are *no* 'events' in any sense of the word as it is commonly used, and only our linear perceptual set allows us even to imagine that there are. The only 'events' that occur do so in our minds; the dynamic happening of the universe is far too complex to be meaningfully categorized into events (recalling Thomas Edison: 'We do not know one millionth of one per cent about anything').

There is only one event, and that is the totality of existence – the universe. Everything we perceive as an event is merely a manifestation within our spectrum of awareness that the universe is happening. To see events as isolated is a false perception; they are merely related more or less tenuously to other aspects of the continuum of which they are all part, and of which each of us is part. There is an infinitely complex interaction among the 'events' we perceive. This interaction is not described within the anthropomorphic simplification of cause and effect. The ultimate reality is that discrete causes of single events not only cannot be identified; they do not exist.

One ramification of the linear cause/effect perception of reality is the tendency to view the present in a fatalistic, deterministic manner: given all we know, it is inevitable that the present should be as it is and the future as it will be; the present is the result of an inexorable sequence of causes and effects grinding their way to the status quo of which the future will be a mere extension. This is an arrogant and cynical view of reality, although those who espouse it talk proudly of 'just being realistic'.

It has been stated that none of us knows enough to be a cynic. 'Realism' is simply not possible, given human cognitive limitations. In this sense it is the so-called 'idealist' who is being realistic. Idealism is not a choice over realism, nor is hope a choice over cynicism. Idealism and hope are what we are left with when our limitations are accepted and our possibilities celebrated.

In discussing the ultimate reality of events, and our capacity accurately to discern discrete causes and effects, we seem to be talking about words, not reality. In fact, the words we use and their corresponding personal meanings – meaning can *only* be personal – define the limits of perception. What we mean by such words as time, space, cause, effect, event, is critical because our meanings limit our perceptions, and also, therefore, our actions that flow from these perceptions.

We perceive only what we conceive and name; in this regard, the adage 'I'll believe it when I see it' would be more accurately put as 'I'll see it when I believe it'. We are *not* discussing reality here. We are discussing our perception of reality, in the form of meanings and ideas. And we are trying to evaluate these perceptions. The conclusion is that the reality we (culturally) accept is false or critically incomplete, and no one knows what actually *is*.

To accept a false reality as real and absolute blocks the possibility of a continued search for knowledge; to acknowledge the limitations on our perceptions of reality stimulates a continued search for knowledge. To accept a false reality impedes human progress and perpetuates archaic social practices based on a fixed world-view; to accept ignorance of reality stimulates innovation in social practices in a search for more successful ways to coexist with our environment.

Time and space, cause and effect, are important tools as we try to 'make sense' of our reality – they are indispensable, at least for 'now'. But to use these tools well, we must understand their limitations as well as their strengths. And these tools have two key limitations: they are figments of our minds, *not* aspects of reality; and they give rise to other false perceptions while blinding us to alternative perceptual orientations.

If we could keep these limits foremost in our consciousness, establishing them as cultural givens, we could use these constructs as tools for change, not as roadblocks to knowledge. And we could more easily demystify the other conventional assumptions about reality which we have named and which flow more or less directly from the linear cause/effect view of reality.

The universe was created for a purpose

To say that the universe was created is meaningless in that it presumes a prior creator-universe (of mysterious quality), and logically this statement leads to an ultimate, uncreated universe. The persistence of the assumption of 'creation' emerges from the common-sense conviction that what is must have a cause. The universe, whatever it entails, is *all* existence, uncreated. It is an infinity of possibilities in process, with no 'purpose' but to be.

The human is the keystone of that purpose, and its ultimate creature

The human is not the keystone of the universe, nor its ultimate creature. Humankind is of the universe at this 'time' and in this 'space', one of the infinite possibilities evolving as part of the universal process. There is a very high probability of more complex and successful possibilities evolving in some place at some time – past, present, future – although it is unlikely that this eventuality will impact at all on our own destiny (although there are those who, in their steadfast adherence to a faith in alien visitations, believe that it already has).

Humankind is master, by intent of creation, of all other existence

Humans are not masters of our own existence, let alone that of all other existence. We have neither the knowledge nor the tools of a master. We are generally ignorant of the specifics of our own reality and that of our immediate environment. We are virtually ignorant of the vast reality of our 'known' universe. We are blind to the possibilities past, present and future of the evolution of the universal process.

Humans have a 'nature', static and immutable

Human nature is neither static nor immutable – this would be the antithesis of existence in process. Immutability leads to the final stage of extinction; it is not a nascent characteristic of a new species. Each individual is born with characteristics, qualities, capacities, based partly in biology and pre- and neonatal environment, which could be termed that individual's 'nature'. What we become, however, is determined by innumerable variables which interact with the characteristics and potentialities intrinsic at our conception. Each of us is a possibility in process, and the potentialities are virtually infinite, although socio-cultural and physical (environmental) circumstances most often severely curtail the exploration and exploitation of our potential. This fact, however, is a statement about the human environment, not about human beings.

When we speak of 'human nature', we are dealing with one of the most crippling lies of human culture. A nature common to all humans past and present could be based only on a crude genetics devoid of any intervening variables, and immune to change.[2] The 'nature' of humankind – as of all creatures – is to change, to evolve, and in a very real sense 'Human' is not an entity but merely a name we give to a specific and limited stage in an evolutionary continuum. Even more than other creatures, humans have no static nature, merely characteristics which pertain at conception to individuals, or groups of individuals, as a result of biological and cultural heritage. The most significant and most prevalent characteristics of humans are the ability to acquire extragenetic knowledge, and the ability to act intentionally to realize a 'vision' – characteristics which, as I demonstrated in Chapter 5, imply a radical venture in individuality, liberated from the bonds of stultifying ideas about 'human nature'.

Two crippling effects emerge from the concept of 'human nature'. First, the concept de-emphasizes the central role of environment and circumstance in forming the individual; as a result, 'human nature' is often seen as the 'culprit' in many of the pervasive problems (war, poverty, crime, ignorance, squalor) that are endemic to modern society. This conviction deflects society from focusing on the critical influence of the political and cultural milieu and societal circumstances in which the individual is immersed. Because a base and static 'human nature' is seen as the root cause, these problems are seen as 'natural' and insoluble. Second, the concept of 'human nature' promotes a rigid, stultifying, non-creative mode of education and socialization, the purpose of which is to mould the individual to acceptable patterns of behaviour – to keep individual 'nature' in check – rather than exploit and develop the individual creative self.

Humans are subject to immutable natural and moral laws

Associated with the lie of 'human nature' is the perception that the universe is predicated on some simple, identifiable natural law (physical *and* moral). If science has achieved any major breakthrough for humankind, it is the realization that physical laws are definitions of human perceptions (knowledge) of cause and effect, and the contingent and extrinsic relationships of matter in this time and space. The physical laws observed by science are definitions of *the present limits* of knowledge, not the absoluteness of knowledge. And these laws are subject to (and do undergo) significant, often diametric, change as our perceptions of natural phenomena change.

It is not the scientist who is the advocate of natural law – it is the mythmaker and the priest. True, science strives in its quest for understanding, in its search for 'laws' which obtain in our time and place. But the genuine and independent scientist knows that she is forever bound by the extreme limits (and subjective nature) of her mind and senses, and the extreme limits of her experience within a virtually infinite cosmos. Jacob Bronowski asserts:

> The laws of nature cannot be formulated as an axiomatic, deductive, formal and unambiguous system which is also complete. And if at any stage in scientific discovery the laws of nature did seem to make a complete system, then we should have to conclude that we had not got them right. Nature cannot be represented in the form of what logicians now call a Turing machine – that is, a logical machine operating on a basic set of axioms by making formal deductions from them in exact language. There is no perfect description conceivable, even in the abstract, in the form of an axiomatic and deductive system. Any finite system of axioms can only be an approximation of the totality of natural laws....
>
> Of course we suppose nevertheless that nature does obey a set of laws of her own which are precise, complete and consistent. But if this is so, then their inner formulation must be of some kind quite different from any that we know; and at present, we have no idea how to conceive it. Any description in our present formalisms must be incomplete ... because of the limitations of language as we use it ... in its logical insufficiency ... it is the language that we use in describing nature that imposes ... both the form and the limitations of the laws we find.[3]

It is important to note that the most common clue that leads science to 'discovery' is an exception to, or inconsistency within, a previously codified physical law. The flaw in the application of the law tells the scientist that she is close to another frontier of the universe of human knowledge. The universe in the hands of the scientist expands, and the 'laws' change. The authentic scientist looks not for immutable laws, but for the universe, and it is the knowledge that the 'laws' are infinitely imperfect and temporary that guides the search.

The concept of natural *moral* law finds its roots in the myth of an absolute natural order, moral in its conception in the mind of a creator – god or gods. The ethics of the god(s) are the moral laws of humans, just as creation follows immutable principles which are the physical laws of nature. Moral law is expressed in terms of 'good' and 'evil'. These terms can be nothing but value judgements subject to change, which have no existence except in the minds of humans and the laws of their societies. There are no actions of any *intrinsic*, universal value. Humans merely judge the value of an act by the prevailing perception of the desirability or undesirability of its effect. Some of these value judgements are long-lasting and almost universal in application; others have a relatively brief life span and are very local in acceptance and application.

Human destiny is predetermined

Following almost inevitably from this concept of natural law is the perception – that is, the belief – that human 'fate', and that of the earth and the universe, are predetermined, and are even following a supremely authored plan. Natural laws determine events and effects in an endless sequence, and there is nothing to be done to alter or influence this inexorable sequence as it unfolds. What happens has to happen because it is the result of natural law; since the law cannot (by definition) be 'broken', whatever happens is inevitable – we know it had to happen because it *did* happen. This destructive fatalism justifies virtually all events that befall us, and obscures the human choice and agency that almost always lie at the root of social evils,

History is linear

The prevailing linear view of history flows from this perceptual *Gestalt* as well. Conventional histories are a deadening misrepresentation of the phenomena of the past and the process of social evolution. The general view of history is that 'events' are causal and linear, and that history can be traced as a chronicle of the line of 'great' men (almost solely men) and empires. Human history is represented as a long series of political events, dates and movements – a veritable parade marching into the present and now marking time until this present is passed – and past – and falls into line.

Such a perceptual set is debilitating. It deadens our capacity to see even the outline of the incredibly complex and dynamic multi-dimensional grid that would, of necessity, characterize a history that even begins to describe the duration of human society. The 'set' is caused by 'History', which is ethnocentric and patriarchal, culture-bound, nationalistic and, in essence, mythic in its form and content. 'History' provides the societal function of institutionalized propaganda, rationalizing the status quo by expressing it as the culmination of an orderly line of events.[4] It reinforces societal values and attitudes and structures, the genesis of which it seeks to explain. It attaches to these elements of the status quo a significance and sense of destiny that seriously impede the development of critical awareness of the society it is 'describing'. Many of us have heard the comment: 'How can I believe history? It is written by the winners.' History feeds nationalism, and corresponding xenophobia, cultural parochialism, racial and religious bigotry, and, in general, represents the classic 'Big Lie'.

This is not to say that histories are the result of a concerted conspiracy of conscious and evil men (although in many cases this has been exactly the case). Rather, our perceptions of the past are determined by our sociocultural orientation to reality. How we see and analyse our past will, of necessity, be determined by our preconceptions about the structure and the components of reality. In turn, our History will reinforce our preconceptions.

The explanatory function of history is that of myth, not of science. It explains the past in terms of the present, not the present in terms of the past. Conventional wisdom forms history, not the reverse – and conventional wisdom too often sees the present as the culmination of a linear progression of seemingly inevitable and predetermined events. This is a critical issue in the activity of humankind. Even if there were natural laws which determine the process of universal existence, the virtual infinity of time and space relative to the human frame of reference ensures a virtual infinity of possibilities evolving, since one obvious principle of universal existence is variety and change. What humankind and this earth become, and what humans do with their universe, is virtually open. And humans are agents, subjects, as well as objects in the process.

Our environment moulds us, even determines us; we are prisoners of the environment. But, as we transform the environment which determines us, we are free – agents of process, the authors of our own destiny. Because of our consciousness, our reflective capacity to objectify the world and create intentions for the future, we have the capacity purposefully to alter our environment. However – and this is the critical point – our successful development is clearly dependent upon our becoming conscious of the possibility that we are a species with the capacity to determine our own actualization. For human beings to become rational agents in the process of the universe, we must first be aware that this is our potential.

Here, again, is a paradox. The very consciousness that allows us to perceive our situation infers that we are in a determined and interminable situation, and that we are the objects, fatally, of that situation. We do not perceive that we are not only in, but part of, our situation, and that our actions in and on that situation change it and its effects. We do not see that we are not mere spectators of our situation, but to a large extent − not absolutely, since the interaction is dialectic − we can be the creator of ourselves and our situation. This consciousness prevents us from fully appreciating our role as the agent of our own existence, of our own situation, and we are unable effectively to bring our subjectivity and rationality to bear on determining our destiny.

We could become the authors of our being and our destiny. We could analyse our potential, analyse the determining aspects of our situation, and choose to act on and with that situation to promote the actualization of our potential of personal vision. If we could do this, and do it together, we could also to a large extent (to *what* extent we cannot know − yet) direct our own possibility in process with the universe. This is the potential of humankind, and of each person, and the actualization of this potential is dependent upon our consciousness that the potential exists.

In Chapter 7 I explore learning and education as critical factors in developing, or inhibiting, this quality of consciousness, and nurturing the transformative capacities of each one of us to be creative and active participants in the social and political life of our communities and the wider world.

Notes

1. Stephen Hawking has popularized some of these paradoxes in his best-selling *A Short History of Time* (1988). It is a commonplace among publishers that this book, by one of the twentieth century's most brilliant mathematical physicists, is one of the most surprising best-sellers of all time, and perhaps also the least read.
2. The politics of genetic theory has been cruelly influential in this century, in justifying discrimination, repression and genocide against various peoples, not only in Europe through the Nazi ideology − the defining event of the century − but throughout the world, North and South. It is a theme that demands constant public outrage and debate. R.C.

Lewontin offers an important introduction to what is at stake in the scientific realm in *Biology as Ideology* (1991).

3. Jacob Bronowski, *The Identity of Man* (1965), supplement on 'The Logic of Mind', pp. 124–5.

4. In this context, it is wise to remember Pierre Trudeau's response to criticism of his government's performance: that the universe was simply 'unfolding as it should'. The positive aspect of this statement is that it was so incredibly blatant that it became its own irony, and entered the Canadian lexicon as a cliché.

7

Imperatives for
Modern Education

Whereas banking education anaesthetizes and inhibits creative power, problem-posing education involves a constant unveiling of reality. The former attempts to maintain the *submersion* of consciousness; the latter strives for the *emergence* of consciousness and critical intervention in reality.... In problem-posing education, [people] develop their power to perceive critically the way they exist in the world with which and in which they find themselves; they come to see the world not as a static reality, but as a reality in process, in transformation.

Paulo Freire, *Pedagogy of the Oppressed*

Education is *the* essential societal institution; in a very real sense, the function of society is education. The effect within society of education is profound and pervasive, and all societies privilege education as the keystone of stability, security, growth and power. As we have seen, it is the knowledge and consciousness of the individual that determine the expression of human potential, and the status of human societies. It follows that as activists we should subject the consciousness-forming institutions in our societies to critical scrutiny.

In my experience as a learner, as an activist and adult educator, and as a parent, education is only peripherally related to learning, and that relationship is largely incidental and often counterproductive. The process of education generally used in homes, in schools, in churches and in other institutions perverts what the human individual is, what learning is, and how the individual person happens to learn.

Learning is an individual, subjective, inventive and dynamic process, within which we acquire the skills, knowledge, attitudes, perceptions and behaviours that define our interaction with the world. Education, on the other hand, is systematic social action to direct this essentially undirected (though not necessarily non-directive) learning process 'productively', to achieve social goals. I do not merely mean schools, although the role of 'schooling' is significant. I also mean parenting, religious indoctrination, and the activities of a broad spectrum of other institutions and media which, at least in part, are intended to influence what and how people know.

Education *could* be self-directed and de-institutionalized – remembering G.K. Chesterton's jibe that his education had been interrupted by so many years of schooling. Education *could* be the systematic action of the individual to direct the content and process of his or her own learning, but this is rarely the case in practice. Education has become a synonym for 'schooling' – in general, *bad* schooling – a phenomenon exhaustively analysed by a host of social theorists and progressive educators.[1] As a term, it is a label for actions directed towards learning, and a label for knowledge or certification that has apparently flowed from these actions. But education is *not* learning. Learning takes place in people's minds and bodies, not in schools, and is accomplished by people themselves, not by schools.

In this context, education has become the institutionalized *regulation* of human learning. An 'education' is the formal training achieved within an institutional context, and the certification by society that we have undergone a prescribed educational regimen that qualifies us for some position, or invests us with some relative status, within society. In a sociological sense, education is the systematic action of a society to ensure that its members know what is deemed necessary if they are to be 'useful' members of that society. The roots of education as a social institution lie in the need for stability and security within societal groups. In this sense, education has traditionally been an agent of the status quo, not an agent of change. In earlier eras, the fundamental and crucial goal of education was to perpetuate the societal group and its traditional survival mechanisms at a time when the line between survival and disaster, between propagation and extinction, was a thin line indeed, and a line over which human beings exercised very limited control in the face of the vagaries of nature. Rooted in a static perception of a static reality – essentially magical and mythical – and the whole gamut of fallacies that flow from this perception, such education does not nurture the free potential of the individual, nor does it exploit the transformative essence of the human learning process.

Unfortunately, while human environmental – indeed, survival – needs have changed, the concept of education has changed very little. To this day education is a societal institution that works counter to fundamental social change; perpetuates the status quo; expounds a static view of humankind, reality and existence; stultifies learning potential, and is actively counterproductive to human growth and creativity. To become a viable force that enables and encourages each person to participate in lifelong action to make a world that is a healthy, safe and humane place for all people, the processes of education in homes, schools, churches and other social institutions must undergo radical changes – changes that are diametric to present concepts and practices.

This chapter explores the changes in education that are necessary and possible. The analysis is presented in three parts: *Aims*, *Activity* and *Implications*.

Aims: Towards a Democracy of the Intellect

Learning, as a phenomenon, has no aim, merely more or less haphazard results. Education, as a systematic attempt within society to *direct* learning, has aims. These aims, if they are at all rational, will be directed towards 'social good' – that is, the perceived continued health and success of society. Accordingly, these aims will be based upon a complex set of beliefs and assumptions about humankind, the individual and society.

If we accept the assumptions and conclusions in the preceding chapters, we must believe that the aim of education should be the actualization of individual human beings as possibilities in process. Only the achievement of this aim will enhance the probability that humankind itself will continue as a viable possibility. This aim should be directed towards the individual. It should focus on human persons as possibilities, then on human societies, and the human species. The success of humankind rests on the success of the societies – and, ultimately, on the *global* society – we form. The success of society rests on the individuals who constitute society. Inevitably, the success of humankind depends upon the success of women and men as authentic individuals engaging in critical reflection and action (praxis) in a dialectic relation with the world and a dialogic relation with other human beings.[2]

The aims of education, if they are to be realistic and functional, cannot subordinate individuals to their society as objects, or creatures, of society; education should focus on individuals as subjects – that is, *creators* – of society. Furthermore, just as learning is an individual process, unique to each person, the aims of education should be stated in terms of the individual.

The primary aim of education, then, should be to facilitate and promote the development of the capacity of individual persons – and thereby, of humankind, the collectivity of persons – to actualize our potential as viable possibilities in process. This we may call the *generic* aim of human education. What is involved in this aim? A central component must be what Freire has called 'conscientization'. For personal growth, and the growth of humankind, each of us must develop critical consciousness of our essence as possibilities in process, and our capacity to be an agent of our own future and that of our global society and of our world, through transactions with our fellow persons and interaction with our natural and sociocultural environment. Intrinsic to this aim is the facilitation and promotion of praxis – reflection and action to transform ourselves and the world. Education should assist us in developing our capacity to act on and with the world in dialogue with other persons.

On the societal level, the aim of education needs to be cultural transformation as a societal norm. 'Culture' is considered here to be the *Gestalt* of human responses to the environment: perceptions, technology, science, education, behavioural norms, art, law, leisure, governance, mores – all the extensions of the human physical, psychological and visionary self. The aim of education should be that human culture be in a state of constant transformation – and that the various aspects of culture undergo transformation *as the norm* desired, expected and precipitated by the individuals in society and facilitated by the structures within society.

This notion of constant cultural transformation may be difficult for some to accept as realistic, let alone desirable. But what is meant is not 'social evolution' – a slow, haphazard process – nor is 'reform' an adequate term, since reform is essentially a structural rather than substantive process, usually only superficial in its material effect. I use the term 'transformation' because it denotes fundamental, substantive change. And this transformation is 'cultural' because the transformations required are not merely political – or even *especially* political – but involve the entire cultural reality, the integrated totality of human response to our environment, including our social environment.

Radical change, and even the threat of radical change, is usually considered to be a source of trauma. The term 'trauma' is often used in this context, denoting as it does a 'wound' or injury, either physical or mental. The connotation is always pathological. We constantly speak of the 'trauma of change' and 'traumatic changes'. Yet the fact is that human beings can and do cope with, and thrive on, radical change and its associative stress when we see ourselves as direct participants with authentic power to control and direct change and its personal effects.

Stress does not have to be distress.[3] Conflict does not have to be destructive. As we explored in earlier chapters, conflict and stress are essential to personal growth, and to social change. Confronting change, stress and conflict is central to human experience. The notion that we need constancy and stability – often defined as non-change – is a notion that is rooted in the fatalistic view of the world described above. The human person is not born static, closed to experience and fearful of change. Rather, we learn to fear change, and to avoid it. Children thrive on change and novel experience, and are traumatized critically by the crude, aggressive, violent and violating repression of their attempts at freedom of experience, perception and expression, and the heavy-handed imposition of pre-set norms, perceptions and practices. If, as children, our learning experiences promoted continuous cultural transformation as a value, and nurtured our natural inclination to participate in and thrive on change, there would be little trauma attached to living in a society in which change was accepted as a cultural norm.

The irony is that we *do* live in a society where radical change is the norm, but it is neither perceived and understood as natural, nor accepted as desirable and controllable. Establishing cultural transformation as a social value and cultural norm would result in no more trauma than is experienced now in a society characterized by rapid, seemingly incoherent change which affects every one of us, and over which we have virtually no control. The response should not be to avoid change, but to transform consciousness so that we can *transcend* the trauma of change by controlling and thriving on it.

We are not static, and do not live in a static world. Immense changes are occurring, and the velocity of change is increasing. And we are coping with this change. We may not be coping very well, most of us – the mental and physical pathologies associated with stress are all too common, and chemical and psychological escapism and isolation are often used as substitutes for reason and emotion as human guides. But we are coping. We are coping so poorly not because we can't cope with change, and thrive on it and control it, but because our natural capacity to do so has not been nurtured and developed. In fact, our capacity to seek and embrace change has been actively, systematically inhibited.

The response to this reality can only be to nurture our natural eagerness for experience, change and growth; to nurture a critical stance towards the irrational, static and antihuman characteristics of our sociocultural reality; to nurture the skills and attitudes that will allow us to understand, control and direct change in harmony with our vision and in co-operation with others. For such a vision to develop as a concrete actuality, the aim of education needs to be the development of what Jacob Bronowski has called 'the democracy of the intellect'.[4] For Bronowski, this possibility is that *all* human persons will come to possess a creative, critical, active knowledge of who we are and within what situation we are, and that we will attain the skill and the wisdom to use this knowledge with other persons to form our future. Central to Bronowski's vision is that knowledge is 'not a loose-leaf notebook of facts' but, rather, 'a responsibility for the integrity of what we are, primarily of what we are as *ethical creatures*'.

Ethics is the synthesis of knowledge, values and vision that underlies all human behaviour and is the basis upon which we choose action. In a democracy of the intellect, our actions to transform our world would be formulated and initiated and consummated through a dialogue involving everyone. These actions would be based in scientific knowledge, artistic vision, and respect for the sanctity of the individuals who constitute society. And they would be predicated on constantly renewed or reaffirmed ethics authored by each person in dialogue within the community and reflected in society as it evolves.

Bronowski states clearly that he does not mean an 'aristocracy of the intellect', which he considers to be 'a belief which can destroy the civilization that we know'. The democracy of the intellect and the continued ascent of humankind will be possible only 'if knowledge sits in the homes and heads of people with no ambition to control others'. Knowledge cannot be restricted to 'the isolated seats of power'.

The actualization of human persons as authors of our individual and collective future (conscientization, praxis), cultural transformation as a social norm, and the democracy of the intellect: these are the aims of education which flow from the assumptions and analysis presented hitherto. The goals of specific educational/learning activities – for example, learning how to weld, or to read – are more immediate objectives which can and ought to be directly related to, or be a direct expression of, our individual praxis exercised in the context of critical awareness, with respect for the integrity of other people, in an atmosphere of constant change as a positive value, and in a milieu which nurtures the ideal of the democracy of the intellect.

Activity

Education is a systematic endeavour towards human learning. The generic aim of education ought to be the actualization of individual persons, and persons-in-society, as possibilities in process. The inevitable implication of such an aim is that the focus of our activities should not be perpetuation of the status quo, but, rather, the promotion of dynamic change; should not be societal maintenance but, rather, individual development, and *therefore* societal development; should not be truth, but knowledge; should not be certainty, but doubt. The focus should be radical, critical and visionary.

On the societal level, the focus should be on developing an expectation of, a preparation for, and the ability to control ongoing radical transformation within society as a natural, healthy and invigorating norm of existence prevailing in the context of a democracy of the intellect. This is the focus essential to a discussion of activities in education, activities that have two aspects: *content* and *process*.

The content of education can only be the human person and his or her reality in process. This conclusion follows from the recognition that all learning is subjective – self-related. No other learning is possible. Educational activity should start with the individual person: 'Who am I? Where am I going? Whence have I come?' It is only with an understanding of the phenomenon of Self that we begin to understand our relationship with other individuals, and with our environment. The motor of learning is the struggle for survival of our individual self – survival we have defined as the actualization of personal vision. Learning concerns itself only with its Self, the individual person, and therefore our own reality and situation. All learning, no matter how common, mundane or trivial, nor how specialized, esoteric or profound, occurs only as it enhances our understanding about ourselves and the environment that defines us, and furthers the possibility of actualizing – making real or actual – our personal vision of what we and our world might (should) be. And we will learn 'things' only to the extent that they do define our selves with and in reality, and to the extent that the things we learn further the possibility of actualizing our personal vision.

A major flaw in contemporary education is not so much that the content or 'subject matter' is irrelevant to the individual – no knowledge is, in itself, 'irrelevant' – but that it is not seen to be relevant even by teachers, let alone individual learners. Most critically, however, the personal relevance of the content is usually not created – as it must be – by the learners themselves, through personal activity and direct application to their individual lives and personalities. Instead, 'knowledge' is specialized, ossified, categorized into disciplines and subjects, artificially segmented and re-presented remote from the individual reality context, and unrelated – irrelevant – to individual interest. The 'subject' is 'taught', rather than individuals being helped to learn about themselves and their world by creating (inventing) and applying the subject matter within the context of a process of actively exploring their own reality. Under such circumstances, the 'material' will not be – indeed, cannot be – learned in any meaningful sense.

In summary, then, the content of education can be only the individual-in-a-situation-now. This is a generic definition, and it is in the context of this definition that specific content has to be described. In traditional discussions on education we normally catalogue the content to be 'delivered', then decide on the most efficient mode of 'delivery'. The content takes precedence, while the process, always seen as delivery – teaching, not learning – is decided almost as a matter of expediency. It is evident that such an approach is contradictory; the process of education is infinitely more important than the specific content.

In fact, the *process* of learning is the essential substance of the *content* of learning. The content is a person-within-a-situation-now;

and the process is a person-within-a-situation-now, learning about self. It is the understanding of the process of individual learning in a situation, and the exercise of this capacity, that should be the primary content of specific educational experiences. In exercising this content/process, the individual will invent and apply – that is, learn – myriad acts, concepts, attitudes, feelings and skills. But these are incidental to the primary content and process – and are certainly not *the* content, or product, of learning. These facts, concepts, attitudes, feelings and skills are integrated and fluid aspects of the developing human person who is *product in process* of her own learning.

The process of education necessary to achieve such learning includes several essential elements, which we will examine in turn: it will assume a phenomenological stance; it will focus on the integration of constructs; it will be global in scope; it will be based in scientific inquiry and reality-testing; it will be active and creative; it will be artistic and self-directed; and it will be largely group-based.

A *'phenomenological' stance* for the process of education implies that:

- The learner is a subject looking at objects, and relationships among objects, in an environment within which she is an active agent.
- The objects and relationships observed are phenomena that can never be fully perceived and understood, and are ultimately – in *absolute* terms – unknowable.
- Learning is the development through experience of a subjective awareness of the character of reality and the dynamic between reality and self. In learning, we create insights about phenomena and infuse these phenomena with meaning and value; the knowledge (insights, meanings) gained is useful, but also tentative and transitional.
- Learning can be neither imposed nor 'revealed'; it is personal, flowing from our direct experience, and integrated with our subjective awareness of self and reality.

A healthy and effective process of education would be integrative. That is, the process would not look at phenomena in isolation from each other, nor (especially) in isolation from the total phenomenon of each person within her environment. It would avoid fragmentation and segmentation of perception – for example, into subjects or disciplines; it would strive for a dynamic integration of perception of self and reality.

Our environment is not fragmented; it is an organism, dynamic and synergistic – an infinitely complex totality. When we are very young, we naturally experience reality this way, although we soon 'learn' to fragment and filter our perceptions.[5] We can learn nothing in isolation from the *Gestalt* of knowledge we have established from previous experience. Either information is integrated or it is not, and if it is not integrated, it is not learned. 'Facts' may be memorized and catalogued away in the mind, but such facts are not knowledge, and not useful, until we integrate and understand them within the context of our own actions within our physical and social environment.

If we are to develop a critical awareness of reality as it determines our situation, and therefore to develop an awareness of the personal actions necessary to transform that reality, we need to develop a dynamic view, one that is integrated, interactive and fluid. We need to see reality in process, not reality as a collection of static 'things' and isolated but linearly connected events. Therefore education has to be integrated, interactive, fluid, focusing on the whole system of reality, not on its constituent 'parts'. Education must be reality in process, about reality in process.

A significant element in this integrative quality of education is that *the process of education should be global in scope.* Its tone and focus should be *international* and *multicultural.* Our environment is the entire world. Our neighbourhood is the planet; the structure of that neighbourhood is a structure based on nations, and explicit in this structure are alliances, interdependencies and hostilities that are manifest at the national and international level. We can do no less than internationalize the process of education to develop the capabilities and attitudes necessary to perceive and confront this reality.

A multicultural scope and focus and tone is essential because the dominant characteristic of our environment is not that it is 'natural' but, rather, that it is an essentially 'man-made'.[6] Internationally, many of the barriers to understanding and co-operation are bound up in the sociocultural infrastructure and belief systems that define nations. Only by adopting an educational process which is seen as 'cultural action', and which explores the phenomenon of culture through a comparative lens and cross-cultural experience, can the ethnocentric myopia that breeds intolerance and inhibits learning and creativity be expunged, and a new world of open possibilities, new perceptions, and an ethic of mutual acceptance and reciprocity be created.[7]

This process of education should also be *based in scientific inquiry* and reality-testing. Science is both a much-glorified and a much-criticized – and certainly widely misunderstood – aspect of modern civilization, often seen either as the bane or as the salvation of society.[8] It is both, and neither. Science embodies the quest for, creation and application of knowledge. As such, science is doubt, science is question, science is the rigorous examination of reality to transform it. The quest for knowledge is the continuous formulation of questions, the construction of possible answers, the application of answers to reality – and the consequential formulation of new questions.

As we have discussed, knowledge does not equal truth, and the authentic scientist seeks not truth, but knowledge for the here and now. To repeat the observation made earlier: the physical laws observed by science are definitions of the *limits* of knowledge, not the absoluteness of knowledge. And these laws are subject to significant, and often diametric, change as our perceptions change. The scientist looks not for immutable laws, but for the universe, and it is the knowledge that the laws are infinitely imperfect and temporary that guides that search.

It is in this sense that I use the term 'scientific' in the context of educational process. The process should contain, implicitly and explicitly, this sense of the nature of knowledge, this sense of inquiry. But also implicit is an approach to learning that is predicated on keen and open-minded observation, on isolation of fundamental questions and radical problems, on creative formulation and testing of hypotheses within the context of reality. Key to such a process is that nothing is assumed to be true *a priori*, that central to any learning process is the careful identification of all assumptions that tend to support a given view, perception, theory, mode of behaviour or course of action, and that every assumption can be scrutinized and tested by each individual, to be assumed ('taken on') only as a matter of critical choice.

I cannot stress this aspect of the process of education too much. If the only change introduced to modern education were the continuous and systematic identification, testing and choice of 'hidden' assumptions, and if the ability and willingness to scrutinize our assumptions were developed as a habit and faculty of thought in all of us – so that we were able and willing to re-examine, retest and reform our basic assumptions around reality, *and did so* – no other reform would be necessary, as all reform would lead naturally from this. And social transformation would not need to be fomented, as transformation would flow as naturally and as continuously as heat from a fire.

The scientific aspect of the process of education contains another element that is essential, and is integrally bound up with the question of hidden assumptions. Not only is an authentic scientific process based on the sense of knowledge and inquiry described; it should also be based on respect for and active promotion of open investigation into divergent ideas and formulations of knowledge.[9] The process of education should be predicated on the accessibility and examination of radically divergent methods and points of view, in the re-forming of assumptions, with no proscription of views, or of intellectual or artistic works. If we are to be protected from the social application of heinous and harmful ideas, we will be protected only by the ability and willingness of the majority of ourselves and our fellow citizens to scrutinize critically and reject the inappropriate.

It was not merely Hitler and *Mein Kampf* which led the Germans and most of Europe to hell. It was, to a large extent, the vulnerability of individuals, in their inability to reflect critically on the words and actions of Nazism and to turn their reflection into action. The same vulnerability led sane people to allow Churchill and Truman to commit those most cynical of atrocities, Dresden and Hiroshima, and to defend and honour these acts in the writing of history. This same vulnerability spawns all manner of bizarre, stupid, violent, antihuman groups, each of which is a crystallization of individual pathologies consolidated in a manipulative, normative structure. It is not only the lunatic fringe that is afflicted – many time-honoured institutions within the mainstream of society are based on the same vulnerabilities, and virtually all social institutions rely on these vulnerabilities to some extent for their perpetuation.

For the educational process to be scientific, it must be neither prescriptive nor proscriptive. It has to foster active, critical examination of reality in a scientific atmosphere using all possible resources of information and analysis. It would be ludicrous, of course, to expect that a systematic endeavour towards human learning would have no bias, and the bias of the approach I am suggesting is explicit in its assumptions and implicit in its method. This bias is reflected in a view of the world predicated on scientific attitudes, approaches, perceptions, and the core 'knowledge' developed to date within mathematics, the physical and life sciences, and the social sciences. A process of education that is scientific will begin with investigation of what is best known, and move to the more inaccessible. This stress on the scientific character of education is based on the fact that the universe as described by the scientist is not *the* universe – perhaps not even a close approximation – but it is our best present approximation, and it is the one and only description that contains within it the material, the will and the means – the method and process – to develop continuously and transform itself. This is the critical element essential to human survival and progress. It is present in a scientific approach; it is not present anywhere else.

At the same time, it is necessary to root scientific descriptions of the world within observation based in the direct practice of social, cultural and political action. Science is not neutral and objective 'description', practised in isolation from the world. We form our reality in thought, then transform it in action, and from this action comes new learning, new formation and new transformation. Science not only influences, but is profoundly influenced by, history and culture, including prevailing ideologies. This is a critical insight of the postmodernist perspective on learning and knowledge – an essential perspective which, contrary to the misrepresentation of its detractors, is not relativist, apolitical or anti-scientific.

A healthy and effective process of education will be creative and active. It is our personal activities, questions, conclusions, choices and actions that provide the will and the power for learning to happen, and it is these upon which the learning process should be built.

This process of education would also respect and promote the visionary and artistic character of human existence. Nothing marks our uniqueness as individuals as do imagination and vision – the individual as artist re-creating the universe in the mind and in free expression through the 'arts', crafts, media, athletics, horticulture, and the plethora of avenues for expression of vision in the realm of 'recreation' and the realm of 'work'. This aspect, too, is at the heart of the post-modernist formulation, and is an important contribution to the scientific project of human society.

Imagination and vision are the cutting edge of knowledge. Knowledge is derived from the process of forming reality in the mind, then questioning this 'reality' by re-forming it in the world. Knowledge is merely the present answers to the questions of the imagination. While the process of creating knowledge should be scientific, the process of formulating questions and creating a range of possible answers is a function of imagination, of vision – it is an artistic process.[10]

Even more central is the fact that, in a very real sense, anything that can be conceived by the human mind is almost undoubtedly possible and 'true' (used loosely here to mean having some referent in reality).[11] The limits we impose on reality are, in fact, limits to our ability to perceive and re-create reality – limits of the imagination. The artistic function of every individual is to break out of, to transcend, these limits on reality, and to see (create) new limits, new thresholds, new horizons, new possibilities for the process.

We are limited only by our imagination, by our vision. When we study human cultural evolution we see the visionary as the *avant-garde*, the explorer on the frontier. And always the visionary is ahead of 'common sense' and 'conventional wisdom', often a pariah, a threat. The paradoxical tensions of human survival have frequently resulted in the execution of the visionary, who later becomes a heroic giant, a martyr to human progress and knowledge, long after the executioners are forgotten or regarded as footnotes to a barbaric past.

The visionary function, the function of creating in the imagination what does not yet exist in the world, and the artistic function of representing our vision to our contemporaries as art in whatever form – and the possible forms are much broader in definition than what is conventionally regarded as 'Art' – is an essential capacity within all of us. The educational process should nurture and develop this capacity as an integral tool in the repertoire of learning skills, and the exercise of this capacity should be integral to the learning process.

In this respect, the artistic function of the individual should not be regarded as separate, secondary or peripheral – as it is often seen now, merely a quality for leisure and recreation. The artistic capacity is integral to the person, to the personality. If *any* characteristic of the human individual could be designated an 'umbrella' characteristic, it is this one. The function of society, and therefore of education, should be the development of a society of 'artists', in which each of us performs all our roles and functions in the sense described above.

Finally, the process of education needs to be *a group process* as well as an individual experience. The phenomenon of learning is individual and personal. But it is evident that the learning process will be more productive if it involves dialogue and the sharing of perceptions concerning common phenomena being investigated, since dialogue maximizes the variety of perceptions, insights and alternative conclusions from which eventually to conclude an interpretation of the reality under scrutiny. Our learning is enhanced when we have the benefit of a pool of information, perceptions and vantage points, and are exposed to the rigour of debate on conflicting perceptions of reality.

This does not imply that as learners we are bound to a tyranny of consensus; we will reach our own conclusions. These personal conclusions will, however, be broader and more critical if we investigate with others rather than within the very limited confines of our individual perceptions and experiences, and if our personal views and perceptions have been tempered in the forge of dynamic tension within group debate and investigation. Beyond this, an essential aspect of our environment is other people. Since an essential possibility is to act on our environment to bring about change, we have two choices: to act alone on the environment, and therefore on other people, unilaterally, without consultation; or to share action with other people on a common environment, out of a shared or negotiated perception of that environment and the mutually desirable changes. While the second choice, carried out carefully and on a broad societal and global basis, is more difficult, it is also more desirable and more potentially successful.

As discussed earlier, we derive our significance of identity from group interaction, which is essential for balance and health and growth. The group is necessary for healthy learning to take place, and to the learning that does take place. The group is an essential component of both the process and the content of learning, and of education.

Implications

What are the implications of this discussion of educational aims and process? Educators and educational structures need to become concerned solely with assisting people to achieve creative practice of their personal capacities in the context of social reality. Schools, in whatever form schools persist, should facilitate learning of reality-in-process: human beings in our environment. The mode should be investigation of the universe to identify 'untested feasibilities', within the limits of reality: to discover what *is*, and what *could be*. Intrinsic to this process would be the exploration and testing of feasibilities through intervention within the learner's environment. Education should be the active practice of creative freedom in which each individual is seen as an untested feasibility, a possibility in process, discovering and testing the limits of reality.

This process would make use of existing information and skills available through study and practice of the natural and social sciences, through mathematics, technology and the arts. But the emphasis would change diametrically: these fields of human knowledge and creative activity would be tapped by choice, by individuals acting as the primary agents of their own learning, to help them solve theoretical or practical problems posed by personal investigation of their environment, and to help them learn skills, or arts, to develop talents with which to express their authentic selves within the sociocultural milieu. Learners would tap the raw material of existing knowledge not as capital to be banked, or as barriers to be hurdled, but as insights and talents and skills to augment and actualize their personal vision as they interact with the environment and the human community.

The means of tapping existing resources would be greatly varied along a broad spectrum of structures, formal and informal. The total environment would become 'the school', the community the resource centre, the present schools merely the home base. The role of educators should be primarily to assist the learner in discovering effective means of acquiring specific knowledge or skills.

It is obvious that the concept of evaluation must be radically transformed, to become an ongoing integrated aspect of the learning process. This element, such a critical and controversial factor in present educational practice, would become a central skill of each learner, a constant guide to the effectiveness of current activity and to the necessity, or desirability, of activities chosen in the future.

Finally, this process must come to be seen as inevitably lifelong and continuous. No longer can we fragment education into primary, secondary and tertiary and adult phases – the butterfly theory of education ('Next year I will attend the Chrysalis, and hope to have my Bachelor of Metamorphosis by 2001'). This process should begin with the assumption that human learning begins at conception and continues to the grave, with no 'end', no culmination, no matriculation, not even clearly identifiable stages (although the crucial formative years should be exploited fully and wisely).

The process of learning is the process of life, and the preparation for a full life is the preparation for full and dynamic lifelong learning, development, change and action. The education of children and adolescents is not the moulding and transformation of a 'child' into an 'adult' – it is a development of authentic, creative human autonomy which continues unchecked if the nascent qualities and capacities are nurtured. This imperative was widely proclaimed by UNESCO over twenty-five years ago, in *Learning to Be, The World of Education Today and Tomorrow* (1972),[12] one of the most clear and far-sighted documents ever produced by the United Nations. This document, the final report of the International Commission on the Development of Education, explored the kind of education required worldwide to move human society towards a humane, equitable and just world. Also known as the Faure Report – after Edgar Faure, the chairperson of the Commission – this report could very well be dusted off and reissued by UNESCO to celebrate the beginning of the new millennium heralded by the twenty-first century. It is an exciting and visionary treatise, and the challenge it offered the world a quarter of a century ago, and its prescription for humanizing education and society, still define a noble and profound project which – relying on funds diverted from military spending alone – could occupy the nations of the world for generations.

If the potential for human learning were not thwarted and perverted by current educational and socialization processes, we would all remain children in terms of our willingness and ability to learn, our acceptance of change, our wonder at life and nature, our openness to new experience. It is for no less an aim than this that we must bring about a radical transformation within present-day educational structures and processes.

The factor to be changed is that education and socialization as practised in virtually all societies on earth – I am not aware of any exception to this generalization – is domesticating, stultifying, anti-human and violent, in the sense that it violates personal sanctity, integrity and potential. This needs to be changed, so that education and 'socialization' become the facilitation of the development of individuals as authentic possibilities in process – that is, critically aware of our individual rights and capacities for creative authorship of personal destiny and creative partnership in the destiny of human-kind, and skilled in the practice of these rights and capacities.

Such a change would ultimately involve not merely the formal educational system. It would involve all institutions, activities and 'tools' that are instrumental in the systematization of human learning and, in fact, virtually all social phenomena related to learning, communication, creativity and production. The discussion here has focused on 'schooling' and parenting, because these are the activities with the most obviously direct effect on the early development of human individuals. Parenting and schooling, however, do not occur in a social vacuum, especially in this age of media saturation. Parenting and schooling take place in a cultural context and a social milieu which exert a pervasive and profound influence on individual development and expression. It is this cultural context and social milieu that must ultimately be transformed.

What is necessary to begin such a transformation? In brief, we need to cease doing violence to our children, and cease to allow schools to do violence in our name. We need to insist on, and involve ourselves in, a new education for a new person.

Parenting can be considered *the* most essential social role, and the effect of parenting the most dramatic and enduring factor in the development of the individual. There is considerable evidence that the basic paths of personality development are well established within the first four to six years of life, and that a radical departure from these paths in later life becomes increasingly difficult to accomplish. Certainly the basic attitudes and stances of the person in her relationship to and with the world are firmly rooted in early childhood, especially the preschool years.

Given this crucial developmental period, it is imperative that parents evolve and practise means of providing children with a dynamic and creative domestic social and learning environment, consistent with the natural learning process and potential. This involves not only analysing, refining and remaking the domestic milieu as a garden for human growth, and a climate of love and authentic interaction. It also involves the active promotion and facilitation, through community action, of effective parenting, activism in the realm of a formal codification of human rights for children and adolescents, and the promotion of humane, respectful treatment of children throughout all societal institutions and structures.

There are signs that profound transformations in parental attitudes and practices are already occurring. Such transformations should not stop at the school doors. As parents we can become the active partners in education, ensuring a continuity in the development of our children, and promoting the healthy and creative environment we believe children deserve and need. And by becoming more actively involved with the school system, we can begin to work to transform the relations and processes implicit within it.

Such direct involvement can be as intimidating as it is imperative. A very close friend of mine agonized that while she was deeply concerned with the overt psychological violence perpetrated by her son's teacher (in Grade One!), she feared making 'a fuss' because of the permanent adverse effect it might have on the treatment accorded her son for the remainder of his stay at that school. We agreed that while the possibility of adverse 'centring-out' of our children was a reality, the battle must be joined. There is too much at stake, not only for our children, but for the entire generation. In the long run, our children will benefit from the experience of seeing their parents 'fight' for them and for essential principles. They will learn, and any temporary pain will never be as serious or damaging as the constant numbness, alienation, and often crippling learning which is the inevitable product of present practices.

This is a perfect theatre for what I have referred to as an 'open conspiracy', an open call to collective action, because action now is imperative, and sane, and healthy; a call for people to join together in bearing witness to their own vision, sharing with others, daring to confront conventional irrationality, and inviting others to participate. For parents, that is exactly what the challenge is.

In the matter of schooling, educators also need to confront reality. Teachers have to learn that their allies are not necessarily within the teaching fraternity and the educational establishment. Their allies are the students and the parents, and those teachers who demonstrate critical respect in their practice. Teachers can no longer hide behind rationalizations about 'the system' and 'professionalism'. As individuals, teachers can cease activities that violate the personal integrity and individuality of students, activities that are domesticating, alienating, failure-breeding, dehumanizing. Teachers can cease to tolerate the filter function in an elitist system. They can begin to practise what they know: no more mere delivery of content, and testing of memory. Teachers can begin to concentrate solely on helping individuals to learn how to learn, how to grow, and how to act on what they know to create the world they want. And in helping to create learning experiences with students, teachers have to reject the myth of neutrality in education. They must commit themselves to the declassification of the content and context of learning. This means, especially, the incorporation of a full-scale international, multicultural and interdisciplinary character to learning experiences. It means a commitment to defy censorship of ideas and modes of expression, and to promote their free exploration. Teachers need also to commit themselves to authentic student-directed learning, a concept that implies both direct participation in creating the curriculum and the use of evaluation as an intrinsic aspect of the learning process, controlled by the learner and devoid of competitive and punitive connotations.

Young people also need to be involved in the transformation of educational structures, and parents and teachers should be their active allies in this endeavour. Young people should be able to assert their fundamental right as free individuals to be the agents of their own learning. Students should practise absolute intolerance (and be supported in this intolerance by parents and teachers) of all forms of authoritarian, paternalist, sexist, racist, ritualistic, prescribed, competitive educational practice. Students should assert their creative freedom, and do so with their fellow students, acting as a collective to protect and promote the rights of all. This means, ultimately, that students have to become full and direct participants in the sociopolitical processes of the educational setting, full partners in the governance and administration, the decision-making and the practice, of these institutions.

Some might label the imperatives presented here as idealistic, radical, even dangerous. They are right on all counts. If we could develop a process even close to that described here, there *would* be learning of a quality and quantity much beyond what is generally considered acceptable, let alone possible, today. The process would be characterized by a rigour and vitality unimaginable in any but the most experimental of today's educational institutions, based as it would be in the intrinsic motivation, the creative artistry, of the individual learner. And it would be successful in developing individuals who represent the antithesis of our present sociocultural norms and structures. They would be free, open, learning, wilful individuals, committed and able to practise freedom and create culture.

I have gone so deeply into the characteristics required in a new approach to promoting and directing institutionalized learning because, as I stated at the beginning of this chapter, the effect of education within society is profound and pervasive, and learning and education are such critical factors in developing, or inhibiting, a free consciousness, and nurturing the transformative capacities of each of us to be creative and active participants in the social and political life of our communities and the wider world. For this reason, any fundamental challenge to the consciousness-forming institutions of our society such as I am describing here, elements of which have long been proposed by progressive educators, will be resisted and undermined – not because this approach is idealistic, and will not work, but precisely because it *will* work and, if implemented, would be a threat to the prevailing social order. As such, the resistance of vested interests will be extremely difficult to overcome – a very precise example of why a *conspiracy*, an *open* conspiracy, is required, in this arena and so many others.

In the forming of a local conspiracy for social change, the elements of learning and education that I have highlighted in this chapter are as relevant to adults, and adult activists, as they are to our children and future generations. Our own adoption and application of these processes – our own 're-education', if you like – can be a first step in relearning how to act with sanity and health in an often insane and unhealthy world. I explore this proposition more in Part III, along with some mechanisms and strategies to empower ourselves while we begin to undermine the power and inhibiting control of prevailing social institutions.

Notes

1. The Related Reading list at the end of this book cites several relevant examples.
2. I rely here, as elsewhere, upon the terminology of the late Brazilian educator Paulo Freire. The conceptualization does not originate only with Freire, but he has been most influential over the past thirty years in propagating the analysis, which is a synthesis of neo-Marxian liberation theology and radical humanist thought. For a fuller appreciation of

'praxis', the reader may wish to refer to Freire's *Pedagogy of the Oppressed* (1972) and Antonio Gramsci's *Prison Notebooks* (1971).

3. For an examination of the concept of stress, see the writing of Hans Selye: *The Stress of Life* (1996); *Stress Without Distress* (1974); and others. Rollo May, in *Power and Innocence* (1972), offers insights into the phenomenon of 'power' in human health.

4. The possibility and imperatives of a democracy of the intellect form the natural conclusion for Bronowski's *The Ascent of Man* (1973), as explained in the final chapter, 'The Long Childhood'.

5. There are dramatic differences in the manner in which 'reality' is perceived among different cultures (as seen in the distinction between the 'linear' and the 'mosaic' perceptual modes). There is much to be learned from comparative sociology and anthropology about the extent to which our perceptual modes are culturally constructed. There is also immense potential in cross-cultural immersion as an educational experience to bring about renewed and critical awareness of self and sociocultural reality.

6. As Marcuse points out, for example, in *Counter-Revolution and Revolt* (1972), pp. 74–8, the environment is entirely too much made by *men*, a fact which the authentic liberation and empowerment of women may finally rectify, to the benefit of everyone.

7. Piaget's discussion of this element of internationalism in *To Understand is to Invent: The Future of Education* (1976), pp. 128–42, is valuable.

8. This has been at the core of the sound and fury generated in the debate on Alan Sokol's now famous satirical prank, 'Transgressing the Boundaries: Towards a Transformative Hermeneutics of Quantum Gravity', published as a serious 'postmodernist' tract in the reputable cultural studies journal *Social Text* (Spring/Summer 1996).

9. An indispensable treatise on this theme is Paul Feyerabend, *Against Method* (1975).

10. Bronowski on the relationship between science and art, between knowledge and vision, is Bronowski at his most inspiring and most insightful. See, for example, *The Identity of Man* (1965).

11. Joseph C. Pearce offers challenging insights to this aspect of human reality in *The Crack in the Cosmic Egg* (1971), a work in which a potentially profound analysis is weakened by the strangely (and unnecessarily) limited scope of its conclusions.

12. UNESCO, *Learning to Be: The World of Education Today and Tomorrow* (1972).

Part III

The Open Conspiracy

It could be said that the very beauty of the world is what makes life so difficult for us. Did I say difficult? Beauty is the impossible which lasts. We have everything to say ... and can say nothing; that is why we begin anew each day, on the widest variety of subjects and in the greatest number of imaginable procedures....

The silent world is our only homeland. We make use of its possibilities according to the needs of our times.

Francis Ponge, *The Silent World Is Our Only Homeland*

8

The Open Conspiracy:
Allies for Health and Action

We call you to ... work with us in inventing the future.... Let us join together joyfully to celebrate our awareness that we can make our life today the shape of tomorrow's future.

Ivan Illich, *Celebration of Awareness*

In the discussion of humanist radicalism in Chapter 3, I concluded by proposing a 'constitution' for a shared conspiracy of action and transformation: 'I will act, because it is sane, and healthy, and human to do so. We will act together, because it is sane, and healthy, and human, and more effective to do so.' This affirmation is the beginning of open conspiracy.[1]

What is open conspiracy, and how can it be a response to the conditions we have been exploring? In short, an open conspiracy can have two basic functions: as a *reference group*, it can be a retreat in which we are able to reflect and recharge; as an *action group*, it can be an extension of ourselves through which we can practise our freedom through action in society.

Open Conspiracy as a Reference Group

A 'reference group' is a group of individuals who have joined together as a social, emotional, factoral and analytic support network. The group is available for referral of personal/practical problems arising from the work of its members. By 'work', I mean our cultural and/or occupational actions. It may involve the 'job' through which we make a living, but is just as likely to involve a variety of other roles such as parent, community volunteer, politician, artist, association member, special interest activist, or citizen. A reference group helps us to place the ambiguities and contradictions of such 'situations' in a broader context of shared norms, values, assumptions, ideals and sociocultural analyses. This involves: (a) emotional understanding and support; (b) analysis of dilemmas; and (c) identification and evaluation of alternative strategies.

At the beginning of this book we explored the tremendous ambiguity and doubt that confront the conscientious person, and how the contradictions that arise from ambiguity, and our conflicting values and needs, can give rise to a psychology of inertia that traps us and leaves us immobilized, isolated and alienated.

The focus within a reference group is on defeating the encroachment of the psychology of inertia by transcending the ambiguity and contradictions, and transforming the dilemmas of inertia through action. This does not mean *resolving* the contradictions and solving the dilemma. Contradiction and ambiguity are inherent in action, and the dilemmas, as stated above, are the corollaries of freedom. The reference group helps us to 'go beyond' the contradictions, to scale the limits of contradiction and expunge their inhibiting character, and then, through action, to alter the specifics of the dilemma. This action alters the field of action, as well as the dilemmas implicit in social-change action itself. The reference group, by sharing the struggle of reflection and action, lends its moral and intellectual support, thereby relieving the lonely and often alienating character of our individual practice. It adds a dimension of communal celebration of human awareness and freedom to an essentially solitary and existential situation.

In the context of our introductory discussion about health, the reference group provides a reference point for our identity needs and a reinforcement of the conviction that our personal vision is valid, and of value. This goes a long way to balancing the pressure of alienation experienced in a world rife with messages of estrangement, a world which, in being threatened, is threatening.

A reference group helps us to surmount our fear, insecurity, 'failure' – all the so-called 'weaknesses' which, as activists, we tend to repress, and which give rise to guilt and diminished self-esteem. A reference group 'takes for granted' the existence of these emotions and reactions, accepts them as valid and necessary, and helps us to express them, and take them into account in action rather than dismissing them as 'weak', 'invalid', temporary lapses. A reference group helps us to refocus on the *intrinsic* essence of motivation and health. A reference group provides nurturance and support, and from it we gather confidence and strength.

Central to the functioning of a reference group is its factoral and analytic support. In our discussion of learning and education, the element of dialogue was stressed. It is self-evident that, in general, 'our' analysis is going to be more comprehensive and valid than 'my' analysis completed in isolation. In dialogue we have the benefit of a broad pool of experience, knowledge, approach and perceptual orientation. In the process of growth and the practice of freedom, such a resource is invaluable. On the one hand, it dissipates our negative (or positive) fantasies, which impede critical awareness and inhibit action; on the other, it broadens our perspective and understanding, and introduces untested feasibilities that might never have occurred to us in isolation.

The reference group, then, provides us with affective and analytic support. But this is only one element of open conspiracy.

Open Conspiracy as an Action Group

The second and corollary function of an open conspiracy is to be an *action group*, an extension of each of us through which action can be taken within society. Action in and by a group is more effective and self-sustaining. Action is reflection in practice, analysis realized in concrete relations, feasibilities tested. The purpose of action is either directly to change a fact, or to introduce a new fact into a dynamic of facts – that is, a real situation – thereby altering the determining relationships among facts, and ultimately bringing about a transformation of the target fact(s).

Attempts, for example, to bring about a change in specific legal, social or corporate situations by lobbying legislators or others who occupy the seats of power is an attempt at direct change. Such attempts are often futile because most of us do not have the power to influence legal, political or corporate decisions. Therefore it becomes necessary to attempt to introduce new 'facts' into the dynamic, hoping that these new variables will affect, if not effect, a change in the target situation. This can be accomplished if the essential principles of the issues are broadened and exposed to public scrutiny, especially if, by acting as a group, the 'normal' rules of participation in sociopolitical and corporate processes are altered.

This type of action was at the heart of Saul Alinsky's approach to activism, and his development of 'Tactic Proxy' is a classic example.[2] By collecting masses of proxy votes from shareholders in large corporations, his movement changed two key facts: (1) management has absolute power in corporate decision-making through control and manipulation of a majority of voting shares; (2) ordinary citizens, and such groups as religious communities, could not be mobilized to use their voting shares to intervene in corporate decisions. Tactic Proxy altered these two facts, with dramatic effects on corporate and industrial policy.

Another example is the wonderful 'adopt-a-politician' strategy developed in Mexico by Alianza Civica (Civic Alliance, a coalition of over 300 popular organizations throughout the country) in the early 1990s when it began its campaign to break the stranglehold on power of the PRI (Institutional Revolutionary Party) that had ruled Mexico for over seventy years. Alianza Civica decided that one impediment to democracy was the absolute impunity of corrupt politicians within the PRI, and the lack of power of individual citizens to challenge political corruption. It initiated a campaign in which its member organizations 'adopted' specific local political officials, and monitored and publicized their words and actions daily in the lead-up to and immediately after the 1994 elections. Suddenly the fact of impunity was challenged – not in the courts of law, which would never touch these officials, but in the court of public opinion. What had been hidden was now exposed. And the fact of isolation, vulnerability and fear on the part of individual citizens was challenged by collective action to hold elected officials accountable for what they said and what they did. This was a remarkable challenge, and a transformative one, which in part contributed to the historic results of the 1997 national mid-term elections in which the PRI finally, after seventy years, lost its absolute political power in the national congress.

Action, then – whether it is action directly to change a fact, or to introduce new 'fact-variables' in the hope of affecting the dynamic and indirectly bringing about a change in facts – is much more effective and healthy when it is carried out by a group which has shared its values and analysis. This is so for three basic reasons:

1. The group can more easily become visible, more demonstrably assert itself, more effectively generate power. In our societies, the fact of a group is more potent than the fact of an individual.

2. Social action is a process of action and reaction, and its dynamic has cybernetic qualities: action, effect, feedback, analysis, action. When there is a group of individuals observing the effect, analysing the feedback, and choosing new action on the basis of these observations, the potential for creative and effective action is enhanced.

3. Because the action/reaction process can be slow and complex, individuals in isolation are prone to frustration, overreaction, despair and surrender. We are limited by our powers of observation and analysis, our negative fantasies, our insecurity, our alienation and our psychology of inertia. Group action provides a milieu and support system to ameliorate these effects, especially when it is carried out in the context of a reference group as described above. The whole group is more than a collection of individuals; it provides its own organismic resources of health, balance, strength and action.

Open conspiracy, then, has two functions: reference group and action group. There are many examples of partial models for the action component, including the two examples above, Tactic Proxy and Mexico's Alianza Civica. The anti-Vietnam War movement would provide a massive case study, and the anti-nuclear movement is a good example, as are many local environmental groups; there is a plethora of examples on a smaller scale.

We live at a time when 'pressure groups' are so massive and pervasive that they have become 'constituencies'. The electoral process, once geographic in its focus and delineation, is now tending towards factional/social groupings with geographic (local) constituencies remaining merely as a structural means of subdividing each social constituency. These new social constituencies comprise ethnic groups, occupational groups, 'issue' groups (gun control, capital punishment, abortion – all are issues with pro and con groups attached), religious groups, equal rights groups (women, homosexuals, ethnic minorities). To some extent, these groups represent open conspiracies to alter some specific aspect of the established social order, whether it be in the arena of opportunity for employment, access to power, conditions of work, freedom from harassment, equality under the law, legal sanction for or against certain behaviours, practices or groups. Every 'constituency' has a theatre of activity, an issue, however broadly defined.

A limit common to most of these pressure groups lies in (1) the absence of many of the qualities implicit in a reference group, most specifically mutuality; (2) a narrowness of scope; and (3) the absence of a comprehensive and ongoing social analysis. While individual members of these groups share a common issue and a perceived common enemy, there is often considerable divergence in depth, scope and specifics of analysis of the issue in the broader sociopolitical context and, in fact, considerable divergence on the perceived ultimate goal of the movement. There are also often very fundamental divergences on the level of basic values and social vision.

The result is a blunted, essentially weakened strategy, and a tendency for factional dissension and eventual disintegration. While the divergence in assumptions and analysis is inevitable – and, in the long run, essential and healthy – it is the lack of mechanisms and norms for analysis, integration and synthesis of these divergences that is eventually so destructive. Beyond this, the narrowness in scope and deficiency in analysis seriously detract from efforts by the movement to communicate its aims and rationale to members of the public upon whose support success is dependent.

Open conspiracy, as I am discussing it, would be most effective when it is multi-issue, or at least a conspiracy of which the one central issue is the right of all individuals to express and actualize themselves in the practice of freedom to transform their society. It would be open conspiracy against the established order on all fronts that limit personal growth and expression, and restrict the right of the individual to take part in determining his or her own future, and that of society. And fundamental to this conspiracy would be the reference group component – dialogue and mutuality.

I am talking here not of a committee, of a 'cell', of a 'party', but, rather, of the germ of 'movement', a group whose mutual purpose is to learn, to analyse, and to act. The commonality among those of us who participate in open conspiracy would be that we share certain basic assumptions about individual freedoms and the sanctity of the individual, and about human persons, and humankind, as possibilities in process. We share certain perceptions about the intolerable condition of human existence in our own community and through-out the world. We share certain convictions that the local and global amelioration of these conditions, and the success of humankind as an experiment in rationality and ethics, will come about only through our own individual knowledge, choice and action. We share the conclusion that the ability and the will to choose and act is directly bound to human learning and 'education'. We share a vision of a world that promotes health and growth for all people on the planet. And we share a hope that the fundamental transformations essential to our vision can be effected, at least locally, even as we share a fear that our vision and our hope are fatally and fantastically invalid, and a corollary tendency to surrender to the psychology of inertia. As a result, as open conspirators we would share a commitment to each other to assist in our continuous struggle against despair and resig-nation. And we would share a commitment with each other to ex-press ourselves by learning and acting, and growing in dialogue, in attempting to validate our hope and further the chance that our vision will be realized. Finally, we would share our action, 'in the knowledge that all we believe may not be true and possible, merely beautiful'.[3] This is the attitude and approach of humanist radicalism.

In essence, an open conspiracy would be a public celebration of awareness and action, a celebration that would proclaim, profess, present and practise. It would proclaim its vision of human persons as the free authors of our mutual destiny; it would profess its hope in humankind to realize this vision; it would present its critique of conventional assumptions, practices and structures, and the injustices which flow from them; it would practise the testing of feasibilities in the theatre of social evolution. It would be an *open* conspiracy, the assertion of a new fact in the dialectic of social transformation.

The open conspiracy I am proposing could take as its focus human learning, for it is human learning that connects all the factional issues of the plethora of constituencies now vying for attention in our societies. The focus could be the practice of education for personal and societal transformation, a theme to which I will return in the final chapter of this book. The content would be persons-in-their-situation, the process would be analysis and action, the theatre would be the entire society: the home, the schools, the churches, the com-munity, the 'workplace', industry, government, the legal and medical establishment, the media, the arts. The open conspiracy would be each of us learning and acting in the explicit context of our situation and our 'present' issue, but in the broader context of the issue of human freedom, growth and health.

It is a possibility that such a conspiracy, once under way in count-less localities, could become a dominant 'fact' of sociopolitical rela-tions, and that the cultural transformation we have explored in this book will have begun to come into effect – that a democracy of the intellect will have begun to come into practice.

It has been said that politics is 'the art of the possible'. This is the classic mantra of the so-called realist school of political theory, who promote what they advertise as *realpolitik*, or a 'politics of the real'. To the contrary, politics *could* be the art of the possible. His-torically, politics has been the business of persuading people that various – virtually *all* – transformative social visions and courses of action are *impossible*.[4] But what is possible is what is believed to be possible – not as a matter of blind and obtuse faith, but as critical choice. And if enough people share a choice, that choice is not only possible, it is inevitable. As Francis Ponge tells us, 'Beauty is the impossible which lasts.'

In Chapter 9 I explore how each of us might begin to negotiate the limits of the possible to initiate a fledgling open conspiracy in our own specific and concrete situations.

Notes

1. In recent years I have become aware of a quite different formulation of this concept as developed by H.G. Wells in an obscure 1928 mono-graph, *The Open Conspiracy: Blue Prints for a World Revolution*. Wells's for-mulation presumes an infiltration of state institutions by an enlightened elite in order to influence these institutions from within to promote an 'inescapable' programme towards a world federation, a 'World Federal State'. My own use of the idea of open conspiracy is radically different, in that it suggests a democratic and popular strategy to confront and transform, rather than infiltrate, the elitist structures, national and global, which lock the world, and most of its inhabitants, in the present con-ditions. Nothing in the analysis presented in this book should be seen as derived from, or sympathetic to, Wells's vision or proposition.

2. See Saul Alinsky, *Rules for Radicals* (1971).

3. This phrase was used in the naming ceremony for my niece Christine Oldfield, written by her father, to celebrate her birth and welcome her

into the human community. Christine now exemplifies, as an adult, the socially engaged learner and activist who could bring about the transformation called for in this book, as do so many of her contemporaries whom I have met in my work.

4. For a very accessible and valuable critique of *realpolitik* and the realist school in international relations, see Jim George, *Discourses of Global Politics: A Critical (Re)Introduction to International Relations* (1994).

9

Theatres and Strategies: Embracing the Future

We love and will the world as an immediate spontaneous totality. We *will* the world, create it by our decision, our fiat, our choice; and we *love* it, give it affect, energy, power to love and change us as we mold and change it....

What does it matter if our insights, the new forms which play around the fringes of our minds, always lead us into virginal land where, like it or not, we stand on strange and bewildering ground? The only way is ahead, and our choice is whether we shall cringe from it or affirm it.

For in every act of love and will – and in the long run they are both present in each genuine act – we mold ourselves and our world simultaneously. This is what it means to embrace the future.

Rollo May, *Love and Will*

The term 'theatre' comes from the Greek word *thea*, meaning 'view'. It is a place where action unfolds and is viewed. Its contemporary use is bound up with the poles of human expression: war and art, specifically drama. Social activism is, in a way, war, and, in a way, art. I use the term theatre to denote the realm of personal authorship of vision – a drama, if you like, where *all* the players have a role in creating the plot and the dialogue. The connotation of artistic activity is of essence. The peripheral connotation of confrontation and war is inescapable, for that, too, is reality.

I cannot define your theatre or strategies. The definition of theatres and strategies cannot be done for others, alone, in isolation. Each of us must make these choices, and share them with our group. I can, however, share what I believe is possible in terms of initiating the process I am promoting, to concretize some of these abstractions and to assist others to re-create, as their own, the ideas I have presented in this book.

One inescapable conclusion from the discussion to this point is that there is only one fundamental theatre of vision and action: the self – my self and your self. The theatre expands as the self expands to include an ever-widening area of social ecology. Each discrete theatre of action is self-interacting with specific phenomena in the sociocultural milieu. The theatre may involve many issues, or one issue; that is, it may involve many facts to be changed, or merely one fact. How the theatre is defined is a matter of scale and of scope.

On the grand scale and with the broadest scope, the ultimate theatre is Self $\longleftrightarrow$ Society; the issue is our freedom to grow and express vision in social action; and the fact to be changed is that present societal relations, structures and dynamics (global/national/local) are oppressive and repressive of our human freedom and growth.

It is possible to create a comprehensive and coherent hierarchy of theatres, from macro- to micro-theatres. This can be useful to establish a philosophical and perceptual context in which to place our actions, and with which to identify principles and priorities. Such an analysis has to be carried out by each of us individually, and in dialogue, for it to be personally real and practical; and it needs to be a flexible tool, not a manifesto. Such an analysis is neither necessary nor appropriate here. But it may be useful to represent a rough schema of theatres which could be central to initiating an open conspiracy group.

There are four distinct, but progressive and cumulative, theatres involved in the process of creating a functioning group.

Theatre One: Self $\longleftrightarrow$ Self

Issue: Health and Action.
Fact to be changed: I cannot act; I am not happy; I am not healthy.
Strategy: Make the bet![1] Choose.

The strategy in this theatre is to externalize our vision rather than internalize the external dilemmas we confront. Decide that you *will* act regardless of the probability of grand effects. Choose to be an artist creating a meaningful, flowering human life. Choose to be sane. Choose to be free. Choose to trust yourself and others. In all this, recognize that your motivation is intrinsic, self-centred. Recognize that your fear, anger and frustration, and your joy, delight and exhilaration, are self-centred – *they are you*.

When our emotions remain self-centred we can express them and deal with them; when we project them into external objects and situations – seeing people or situations, for example, as the source and 'cause' of our emotions – we are no longer in touch with ourselves, and external 'realities' will control us. There is a difference between the acknowledgement that we are experiencing fear, and the perception that a specific situation, in and of itself, is intrinsically fearful. In the first case, we can deal with our own fear; in the second, the external situation will continue to control us. Similarly, there is a difference between the acknowledgement that we are bored in an activity, and the belief that the activity, in and of itself, is intrinsically boring.

Pledge to yourself not to be trapped by projection. Pledge to yourself to be slave to no externals: no situation, no ideology, no dogma, no absolute, no system. Choose the 'true testimony of profound non-conformity'.[2] Our only obligation is to our authentic choices, and commitments made to and with ourselves and others.

The central act in this theatre is an act of love – for ourselves and for our fellow human beings – and an act of will. It is *the* existential act: the solitary assertion of free self. I will act because it is sane and healthy to do so. I will *act*, I will *be*. I will.

Theatre Two: Self ←→ Others

Issue: Dialogue and Action.

Fact to be changed: I have no allies, and allies are essential to health and effective action.

Strategy: Seek out others like yourself.

We may be abnormal in our beliefs and our vision, but we are not unique in our abnormality. Within our circle of friends and acquaintances and co-workers, there are individuals who – perhaps privately and silently – share our alienation, our assumptions, our convictions. Within our community there are many individuals, active and inactive, who would thrive on an alliance of love and will. A very large number of people in virtually any community would read what is written here and find very little that was startlingly contradictory to their private beliefs and ideals, and would in fact find it a welcome affirmation.

The task in this theatre is to find these individuals, and invite them to share your choice and risk. Sit down, break bread, celebrate your hope, and talk. Explore your possibilities, your untested feasibilities. Decide whether you are a potential reference/action group. If you are, try it.

This may sound simplistic. The fact is, it is *simple*; but it is not easy. You have to search and, most importantly, you have to risk dialogue. In any case, the task of seeking out potential allies must be carried out simply and directly, and the specifics of the search and the contact will be dependent on the specifics of the situation of each individual.

Theatre Three: Self ⟷ Group

Issue: Reflection and Action.

Fact to be changed: The group is not a functioning reference/action group.

Strategy: If you have carried out, even tentatively, the task of seeking allies, then you and your allies (friends) are at a crossroads. If group dynamics and action were easy, humanist radicalism would already be a significantly more potent force than it is.

You have to solve the problem of dynamics and action for yourselves. It must be your analysis, your process, your creative solution. You are in a learning situation, and your knowledge has to be self-created to be viable. In any case, there is no 'method'. There are various models, but no method. Each group creates itself in evolving its own methods, its own dynamics and process. Anything else would be artificial, extrinsic and short-lived, and before long its energy would be focused entirely on maintenance and self-perpetuation. This phenomenon is tragically common, and can be seen in the histories of myriad activist groups.

While it is not possible to offer a prescribed method, it may useful to identify some characteristics of a viable group – characteristics that need to emerge from your initial activities if you are to coalesce as a group that is dynamic and enduring.

- You need to emerge as a group, or at least a network, of individuals who can provide *norms, nurture* and *support* for each other, in the sense described in Chapter 8.
- You need to emerge as individuals with an authentic and profound *respect for* and *acceptance* of each other. This will not always mean active affection, nor a commonality in all (or even most) things. It does mean 'kinship', and the 'love' that is common to kinship. You will confront, argue and struggle, but this struggle should always be tempered and steered by respect for, and acceptance of, each individual. And this acceptance has to be personal, not an extrinsic, pragmatic, artificial mechanism; it has to be real, not ideal. If this quality is not present within your group, you can hardly expect it to be present within your actions in society, within your relations with other individuals with whom you share mutual action. Without this quality in relationships there is no dialogue, no authentic action.
- You need to emerge as a group whose commonality is the macro-theatre of universal freedom and justice, and the micro-theatre of the personal art of free self-expression. Your essential bond should be that you each need help in *actualizing* the personal affirmation – the act of love and will – discussed above. This is necessary to prevent the motive force of your group from becoming merely extrinsic – the issue, the movement – for if this happens, the group will be at the mercy of the issue and will eventually burn out.
- You have to emerge with a shared set of assumptions, hopes and strategies, focused on 'the possible', on untested feasibilities. This does not mean that all assumptions and all feasibilities must be common. That would be neither possible nor healthy, nor particularly fruitful. What it does mean is that certain basic values and goals need to be common. And it means that divergences in perceptions, beliefs and assumptions must be shared, explored, understood, accepted and/or accommodated. You need to *know* each other to accept and respect each other, and to avoid fundamental dissension in the future when you discover (with some shock) that you are coming from different places and moving towards different goals.

Openness is much more critical here than commonality. Diversity and divergence are absolutely essential for a dynamic growth-centred group. Ignorance of divergences in one another's basic assumptions and perceptions is ultimately more disastrous to a group than the divergences themselves. Not the least of the dangers of such ignorance is that it leads to a fatally uncritical form of analysis, and eventually to inbred intolerance for dissent and confrontation within the group, and towards the community with whom the group is working.

- You need to emerge as an effective *learning group*. As an action group your mortal enemy will be ignorance: of yourselves, of the reality you wish to change, of others involved with the same reality, and of change dynamics. You have to be able, first, to identify what you need to know; and, second, to exploit the resources of the group, and the community-at-large, in such a way that you learn what you need to know in order to analyse and act. Inevitably this will involve a significant broadening of your understanding of scientific, sociological, psychological, cultural, socioeconomic and political realities.

- You need to emerge as an effective 'think-tank'. This means that you will want to create a group that is open, creative and imaginative (in some fashion, 'insane'). You want to be able to arrive at radical conclusions about what is and is not possible at a given point, and arrive at keenly creative and imaginative means to achieve your goal.

- You want to emerge as a group that strives to be an 'open system', accessible and capable of incorporating, in a dynamic way, new people who are willing to participate, and to say farewell graciously to others who choose to move out. You need to struggle against becoming inbred or exclusive. When a group of activists becomes an entity, individuality and personality is often quickly lost, and The Group takes on its own life. A new 'fact' has been created, but it is no longer a possibility in process.

- Finally, you want to emerge as a group characterized by joy, excitement, energy and humour. The process of the group itself must be rewarding and humane. If the group merely implies endless work, motivated by 'cause', with the end some distant ideal, it will be unhealthy, ineffective, and will ultimately disintegrate. Pioneer feminist, socialist and radical activist Emma Goldman is purported to have declared: 'If I can't dance, I don't want to be part of your revolution!' There are few better slogans to guide your group in its actions together.

These are some characteristics of a viable reference/action group. A productive strategy in this theatre will focus on working joyfully to create and develop these characteristics in your group.

Theatre Four: Self in Group ←→ Other Groups

Issue: Activism and Isolation.

Fact to be changed: We are not connected with the activist fact in our community.

Strategy: Define the landscape, and identify yourselves.

There are two factors that make this theatre an important initial outreach for your fledgling group. First, you are going to have to 'get to know the territory' before you can become effective. You need to discover what is happening in your community, and who is doing it. You need to become familiar with the phenomenon of activism and change in your community.

Second, a bitter irony of the sociopolitical reality is that while there is probably more citizen activism – more concentrated, sophisticated conspiring by activist groups – today than at any other time in 'history', these activities remain haphazard and sorely underachieve the goals articulated. And these activities, rather than creating their own momentum and self-sustaining energy, seem to leave in their wake the debris of despair, exhaustion and inertia. The burnt-out activist is a common casualty. Movement is so slow and change so minuscule.

There are many reasons for this. The 'establishment' has become very sophisticated at defusing and co-opting issues. The issues themselves are myriad, and complex. On every issue there are factions whose conflict ranges from subtle distinctions of ideological purity to diametric polarization. All this can cause a loss of hope and energy. The irony of the phenomenon is that most activist groups are trying to convince you and me to support *them* by changing *our* behaviours, and by joining our voices to theirs to change a given fact in society. The success or failure of an activist group lies less in its ability to convince the 'powers that be' to change than in its ability to convince you and me, fellow citizens, to demand change, and to bring it about. That is: their success or failure lies in the realm of education, and in their ability to connect with you and me, and hundreds of others, to educate and motivate us. *Our* inertia is a prime cause of the failure of activism in our community.

In the light of this, one viable strategy in this theatre is for your fledgling group to identify *every* activist change group currently working in your various environments (there will be scores of such groups). When these groups have been identified, measure the merits of their activity – that is, make a judgement about the validity of their goals and mode of action. Then, on the basis of this evaluation, communicate with those groups identified as having goals and approaches consistent with your own, expressing active or moral support for their aims and actions. Whilst you are carrying our this investigation, you can start a filing system and a mini-community resources library, perhaps assigning a certain number of these groups to each member of your group for continued update, research and liaison. What would such preliminary investigation and reaction accomplish?

- You would gain an astounding overview of the current scope and status of activism in your environment, of the plethora of 'issues', and of the vast array of feasibilities even now being brought forward.
- You would consolidate your group through this co-operative task, a task which involves all the fundamental aspects of a reference/ action group: learning, choosing, acting. This provides a context for exploring commonality and divergence.
- You would identify immediate potential theatres for action, and would inevitably establish your own priorities among them and begin to evolve synthesizing strategies.
- In supporting groups whose aims are consistent with your own, you would be reinforcing the commitment of others who need nurturance and support just as much as you do.
- You would be developing an invaluable network of contacts and potential allies.
- You would be setting in motion a process that will be invaluable for providing momentum for the activities of your group. The critical leap from commitment to action would be made.

How long would this take? With a group of eight to ten people who hold down 'regular jobs', it would take about four to six months of hard work in a medium-sized city, or a more far-flung rural region. Even if it took six to twelve months, the effort would be worth it. When the process is complete, you would have undergone a trans-formative action of profound implications. You would be involved in and active within a group, connecting with others in mutual support and action. What you will have learned will help you to carry on and on. Action will be seen as real: it is happening, and we can happen with it.

These are some perceptions on four theatres and strategy orient-ations central to initiating a reference/action group and your own open conspiracy. The discussion should be taken as just that, a dis-cussion, not as a prescription.

In talking with people I have sometimes been struck by the fact that while we seem to be easily captivated by the power of socio-political analysis and the high-purpose strategies for massive and radical social change, when we discuss the more prosaic chore of *initiating* the process – the painstaking, unromantic groundwork of establishing commitment and principles, of group-building and mobil-ization – we somehow experience a loss of spark, of enthusiasm, even of confidence.

This seems an inevitable tendency, and it is one that we must overcome. As I pointed out above, it is at the personal, individual level that activism succeeds or fails. A prime function of the group is to help each individual to continue to act and to grow. According-ly, the degree to which the group has been firmly established and carefully developed is largely the degree to which the group, and therefore the members who constitute it, will be durable and successful.

The matters discussed in this chapter may not seem, on the sur-face, to be very poetic, exalted or exciting. We tend to think that social action campaigns should be more dramatic and heroic. And they can be. But this is where we *must* start, and the task is exceed-ingly difficult. It needs to be done thoroughly, with discipline and with unrelenting standards of excellence and honesty. If it is done, there will be, ultimately, no failure, and dramatic, even heroic action will be possible. Your group, and many groups together, will prevail. If it is not done, however, there is absolutely no chance for us to build sustainable movements for transformation of our society. The challenge is ours.

In the final chapter, I want to explore the type of social education process that could be at the heart of our collective strategies to begin to bring about the changes we envision in the world.

Notes

1. See John Fowles on 'the bet situation' in *The Aristos* (1970). Fowles discusses the dilemmas of ethics, choice and freedom in the context of the inescapable ignorance with which we face the present and the future.
2. Ivan Illich, *Celebration of Awareness* (1970), p. 16.

10

Education and the
Open Conspiracy

The fetishism of the commodity world, which seems to become denser every day, can be destroyed only by men and women … who have become free to develop their own needs, to build, in solidarity, their own world.… [The structure] can be brought down only by those who still sustain the established work process, who constitute its human base, who reproduce its profits and power. They include an ever-increasing sector of the middle class, and of the intelligentsia. At present, only a small part of this huge, truly underlying population is moving and is aware. To help extend this movement and this awareness is the constant task of the still isolated radical groups.

To prepare the group for this development makes the emancipation of consciousness still the primary task. Without it, all emancipation of the senses, all radical activism, remains blind and self-defeating.

Herbert Marcuse, *Counter-Revolution and Revolt*

In this final chapter I will discuss the place and the role of education in the open conspiracy. Just as the critical variable in human success is consciousness and knowledge, so must the critical focus of strategy and the mode of action of the open conspiracy be consciousness and knowledge. And – initially, at least – education must be a pivotal theatre of activity. Education – as true praxis, reflection and action in dialogue – is the hub and the spokes of open conspiracy.

In observing, reflecting upon, and analysing reality with the goal of formulating action strategies, we must always have a focus. Consciousness and knowledge and learning can be that focus. There is an intrinsic connection between knowledge and action. What people *do* is absolutely bound up in what they *know* and *think*, and what they know and think is bound up in what they do. If we wish to transform practice, we have to identify and decode critically what it is that people know and think, what makes them do what they do, and what makes them accept the practices and structures they accept.

In effect, people practise a paradigm. The classic treatment of the affect and effect of 'paradigm' is contained in Thomas Kuhn's groundbreaking book *The Structure of Scientific Revolutions*,[1] and the concept has become very influential not only in the natural sciences but in the social sciences as well, particularly with regard to social-change theory. By paradigm I mean an apparently coherent and comprehensive concept of reality. In science and social science the paradigm is a systematized and articulated model. But even in the commonplace world, every person behaves in accordance with an *internalized* paradigm – a world-view and philosophy of life – although the degree to which it is conscious and articulated is extremely variable. The paradigm that drives most people's activities is considerably removed from the fully schematized, internally consistent and comprehensive models operational in academic and scientific circles. The paradigm of most of us is derived from the structure of society and the home – including the social-political relations implicit in social institutions, and the family – and from the conventional curricula of primary and secondary schools which have been designed to support, promote and propagate the prevailing belief system of the dominant culture. The many gaps and inconsistencies in personal paradigms are usually unseen, and when they are spotlighted they are rationalized with ideology and the intellectual Polyfilla of revelation and forced hypothesis. Most people adopt a 'revealed' paradigm, and accept new information only to the extent that it conforms with the essential truths of that paradigm.

To bring about social transformation, we need to develop an explicit and critical understanding, or 'uncovering', of the prevailing paradigm, identifying the 'keystone' assumptions and facts that we want to challenge, and only then developing change strategies. This is an educational process: What is known? What needs to be learned? How do we facilitate that learning?

The crux of change strategy is that if we are to transform practice, we need to bring about a transformation of paradigm. If we can effect a transformation of paradigm, practice will begin to transform itself. If we ignore the paradigm, only confronting practice with anti-practice, we will produce a clash of practices, and an invisible, unarticulated clash of paradigms, from which will eventually emerge a 'winner' – normally, the most powerful – and usually a brutal suppression of the competing practice and paradigm. Or there is no clear winner, merely conflict, and some eventual and temporary accommodation, the nature and feasibility of which is not a creative product of the protagonists involved. Neither of these possibilities approaches the fullness of human potential for re-creating the world.

It is inescapable, then, that learning and consciousness has to be a critical focus for change strategy – What is the prevailing paradigm? How can it be transformed? And it follows from this that education ought to be one of our primary modes of action, for it is only through liberating education that fundamental transformation of sociocultural practice is possible. Many have concluded, in desperation, that the only way to bring about fundamental change is by forced overthrow of the prevailing political order, transferring power from those who control to those who are controlled, from oppressor to oppressed. History, including very recent history, teaches a different lesson. Those who overthrow power replace it with themselves. They are still faced with the task – indeed, the radical responsibility – of education, the transformation of paradigm and social practice. Unless this is authentic education for liberation and transformation, rather than the dogmatic imposition of new ideology and regulated practice, the transfer of power through political revolution has changed nothing; it has merely replaced the old oppressive system with another.

When we fight violence with violence, violence wins; and when we replace power with power, power wins. The open conspiracy, to be truly transformative, has to seek the transformation of power, not merely the transfer of power. This requires radical, transformative education, practised in advance of and as part of an ongoing social and political process of transformation, in what will be, of necessity, a long, patient and humbling struggle. It is precisely for this reason that we need to conspire openly to effect this strategy – to sustain ourselves, and those who follow us, in this open-ended transformative project.

What are the implications of this? First and foremost is the fact that action cannot be restricted merely to attempts to bring about transformations in the 'schooling' of children. While our children are our hope, *we* are the hope of our children, and the transformations that I have postulated have to be accomplished throughout a broad spectrum of social institutions. It is taking part in that socio-cultural reality through the long childhood of human development that people are 'educated', and this process is lifelong. The schools constitute only one factor, even in systematic learning. The major factor in learning is the impact of sociocultural structures and relations on the growing person, and the inferences and conclusions drawn from this impact as manifested in self-concept and world-view, and in adaptive and creative skills.

To be sure, the school provides a significant *context* for this impact, because so much time in early life is spent there, but the impact is derived from the experience of social structures and relations, not from the indiscriminate and arbitrary content that is scattered almost as we would scatter feed in a barnyard trough. It is society that is the real and total learning environment, and it is in transforming societal structures and relations that we transform our learning environment, including the schools; and a significant aspect of individual learning will be the experience of, and participation in, that transforming action itself.

The necessary transformations apply to all activities and tools that are involved implicitly or explicitly in the systematization of human learning, development and expression. In effect, this involves the bulk of social institutions: parenting and the family unit, schooling, vocational 'training', adult education, communication and cultural media, politics, art, labour, management, the workplace, the market-place, the community – all social phenomena related to human growth, production/creativity, recreation and communication.

This is an extremely broad focus of action, and it is a gargantuan task even to conceive of systematic impact on such a complex and dynamic interplay of forces and phenomena. Even when we have moved past the inertia described above, and are committed to action without guarantee of significant impact in the short term, the inclination is still to fragment and compartmentalize, by identifying discrete elements that can be understood, analysed and acted upon in an intensive manner. Inevitably, at the level of concrete action, this must be done – we all have our interests, experience and expertise, and we have only one life.

We *will* limit the scope of our personal action; we *will* choose our own theatre. The danger inherent in this inevitability is that, in making our choices, we lose our overview, our perception of intricate and complex interplay, and we lose sight of the fact that the entire complex must be transformed eventually, or our own intervention will remain remote and isolated.

We need perceptual devices, if not structural devices, to assure that our personal choice and action are not remote from the choices and actions of others committed to, and working towards, social transformation. We need to infuse the open conspiracy with an isotropic quality, so that the ethics, ideals and strategies, in being charged by common essential properties, are in harmony and concert.

We have already discussed two such perceptual devices: the assumptions of humanist radicalism, and the affirmations of the open conspiracy. In completing this book, I want to suggest a third device, one which is particularly germane to education as the focus of strategy and mode of action.

We have seen that the scope of the issue of transformative education is awesome, and that the institutions involved in 'education' are myriad and pervasive. What is needed is a unifying construct to bring coherence to a complex interplay among phenomena, and to establish a commonality in the theme and focus of strategy. That unifying construct already exists in the concept of 'development education'.

Development education is normally viewed in one of two ways: education *for* development, or education *about* development. The 'development' usually referred to in both these contexts has been the socioeconomic development of nations, particularly those in the Third World, the so-called 'underdeveloped' or 'developing' nations. These contexts are broadening as we gain a deeper understanding of phenomena and issues. The dichotomy between 'developed' and 'underdeveloped' is beginning to be seen as counterproductive, if not false. The concept of development itself is under close scrutiny. The assumption that development is essentially a question of relative economic growth, a matter of production, employment and consumption (standard of living) measured in economic terms against a standard set relative to the most affluent and industrialized nations, is no longer universally accepted as a viable assumption.

On the contrary, development is increasingly perceived as a sociocultural phenomenon to be measured in terms of quality of life, self-reliance, cultural viability and vitality, human freedom, civil and social justice, and equality of opportunity for health, growth and creativity. At the heart of this emerging concept of development is the conviction that development is primarily a *global* phenomenon. And the key to a strategy for global development, as described, is international interdependence, justice and equality. When development is defined in this latter fashion, the concept 'development education' takes on a much broader context and significance, and provides a construct that can define the mode of action for social transformation on the broad scope described above.

In this context, development education can be defined as the development of people with attitudes, knowledge, vision and skills which allow them to participate actively in the development of humankind and a world characterized by global quality-in-life; self-reliance *and* mutuality – that is, interdependence; cultural viability and vitality; civil and social justice and equality; and individual freedom, health, growth and creativity.

Development education does not distinguish education *about* human development from education *for* human development; nor does it distinguish national development from international development, *our* development from *their* development. Implicit in this definition of development education is the conviction that development is a universal phenomenon with an all-or-nothing character. There is only *our* development as humankind – the global neighbourhood.

Development education can be the mode of action for our open conspiracy: education that promotes a transformation of paradigm, and the corollary transformation of social, cultural, economic and political practice necessary for authentic development of all persons and peoples on the planet. If we accept development education in this sense as a viable focus of strategy and mode of action, then it is crucial to recognize that a transformation of paradigm and practice is not effected by 'teaching', by the declaration that some aspects of the prevailing paradigm are invalid and should be replaced by others. R.L. Warren, in examining the implications of Thomas Kuhn's theory of paradigm and scientific revolution, states:

> Although Kuhn does not deal with the sociology of knowledge (in terms of the social-relational aspects of scientific knowledge), his analysis is highly relevant to it, and compatible with it. For he maintains that, contrary to the widely-held impressions, scientific knowledge does not advance through gradual accumulation of new knowledge and correction of

previous error marked by particularly important discoveries. Rather these important discoveries tend to mark discontinuities in the historical process; for a discovery is not merely a new addition to knowledge but characteristically brings with it a new definition of research problems.... A new set of ways of conceptualizing, of relating data to each other, of ways of defining problems, of research techniques, usually accompany such 'scientific revolutions'.[2]

Further on, in discussing his own use of Kuhn's concept, Warren says:

In incorporating Kuhn's concept ... we will make special use of his notion that a paradigm brings with it not only an 'explanation' of a problem, but also a 'reformulation' of the problem in conjunction with the explanation, a re-definition of what orders of data are more or less irrelevant to it, and what methods of research validation are called for.[3]

The connection between Kuhn's theory, its sociological application by Warren, and our own discussion is direct and dramatic. The transformation of paradigm for individuals and for a community is the same process as for individual scientists and the community of scientists; only the scale and the specifics differ. In fact, a scientific revolution has taken place when the great majority of individual scientists in the scientific community have undergone a personal transformation of paradigm and a corollary transformation of scientific practice. A cultural revolution will have taken place when the same phenomenon of paradigm shift, and transformation of social practice, pertains to the great majority of individuals in a sociocultural community – and eventually, we can hope, in the global community.

What is involved in such paradigmatic transformation? Kuhn points out that 'the most obvious examples of scientific revolution are ... the major turning points in scientific development associated with the names of Copernicus, Newton, Lavoisier and Einstein.' He goes on:

Each of them necessitated the community's rejection of one time-honored scientific theory in favor of another incompatible with it. Each produced a consequent shift in the problems available for scientific scrutiny and in the standards by which the profession determined what should count as an admissible problem or as a legitimate problem-solution. And each transformed the scientific imagination in ways that we shall ultimately need to describe as a transformation of the world within which scientific work was done. Such changes, together with the controversies that almost always accompany them, are the defining characteristics of scientific revolutions.[4]

Warren considers a 'discontinuity in the historical process' as the critical element in paradigmatic transformation; for Warren, it is not merely a new *explanation* of a problem, but a *reformulation* of the problem, which involves new definition of problems, new sets of ways of conceptualizing, of relating and researching data.

For our purposes, the transformation of paradigm and of sociocultural practice will be accomplished by the raising of novel questions, the introduction of new data, the postulation of new relationships, the formulation and assertion of new alternative feasibilities. A paradigm change is not merely the assimilation and accommodation of new 'facts'. Rather, it is a transformation of our way of forming reality – the problems we see, the questions we ask, the information which takes on importance and the significance of that information, the relationships we perceive among phenomena, the feasibilities we see as possible and fundamentally important. It is, in fact, a re-formation of self and a transformation of worlds.

This is the power, for example, of such symbols as the haunting photograph of 'Earthrise' from the moon: spaceship Earth, the global island, becomes real; old limits are shattered, perceptual sets changed, and new feasibilities perceived. It is a radical transformation of consciousness 'really' to feel yourself an 'earthling'. It is also the power of another kind of photograph, the Vietnamese child screaming in napalm-pain as she runs to nowhere. The human pain and horror that was an abstraction *becomes real*, and cannot be ignored. Anyone who saw that photo almost thirty years ago *changed*, and will never be the same again.

The scientists Kuhn uses as examples did not merely *state* their theory; they asserted and applied their perceptions in the world in such a way that they could not be ignored. They demonstrated the applicability, feasibility and validity of their vision, and in so doing they gained allies; eventually their theories had to be 'dealt with', and in dealing with their theories, science – and society – was transformed.

The strategy of the open conspiracy needs to be the assertion of new 'facts-in-action' in such a way that they become real and subvert the prevailing paradigm, which rationalizes inhuman practice locally and globally. These facts-in-action, when they are discovered by individuals, will demand new perceptions, new questions and answers; will demonstrate historical discontinuity, and force a reformulation of problems and the reality in which problems are perceived – all of which opens the individual to untested feasibilities, to new ways of seeing and being. The means to achieving this is the development education mode of action, and implicit is a problem-posing, activity-centred mode of education.

The first critical step in such a process is the personal affirmation of sanity and action that we have been discussing. A second critical step can be the formation of reference/action groups. The third step, then, can be the activities of such groups in helping others to acquire 'action-knowledge', and motivating them to become allies in action on some structure or phenomenon. Action-knowledge is knowledge possessed so personally that it must be acted upon; it cannot be ignored. This is distinct from factual knowledge, which is rote information with no personal significance; and perceptual knowledge, which is inarticulate knowledge that *does* affect perceptions, but is not a conscious direct influence on behaviour.

The creation of action-knowledge, and the associated motivation to social action, can be accomplished in two concurrent and mutually supportive ways:

1. Through direct assertion by the group (or individuals from the group) of facts-in-action – such as the fact that corporations and governments *can* be held accountable, as demonstrated by the examples of Tactic Proxy and Alianza Civica in our earlier discussion. Such assertion, as it affects others, can attract allies who are sympathetic to the explicit practice, or implicit assumptions, of this new fact-in-action. This will move them to reach out and explore the possibility of joining in the analysis and the action. Such assertion will also affect those who are hostile or opposed. It is the dialectic between these individuals and the new fact that constitutes the first breath of transformation.

2. Through 'community development', in which the group (or individuals from the group) seek out people who are affected by some structure, phenomenon or social practice upon which the group has decided to focus, and motivate them to take part in an

analysis (thematic investigation) leading to direct action, further analysis and ongoing action.

In both cases, the act of choosing to act with a group to effect change, and the change-action itself, will involve an affirmation and re-formation of self for the new allies, and a transformation of their world in the sense described above. In both cases, the process is educational, and constitutes development education.

As the 'conspiracy' grows, the mode of action will remain educational in character: the assertion of fact-in-action, the gaining of allies, the development of a supportive and change-effective network, transforming action, the gaining of allies, in a continuous but expanding cycle. As the fact of the conspiracy asserts itself, society will deal with it, and, in dealing with it, the social paradigm and society will change. The force of this new fact will become a social phenomenon containing its own transforming force.

What are the theatres for the development education mode of activism? Quite literally, wherever you are. Choosing to take part in open conspiracy means choosing to fulfil all your personal and social roles consistent with a humanist radical ethic – in the words of Ivan Illich, quoted above, to 'make our life today the shape of tomorrow's future'.

In Chapter 7 we examined some imperatives for those directly involved in education and parenting. I suggested that we are all directly involved, as parents, students or educators – even if, for the moment, we see ourselves as none of these – and that each one of us should become an educational activist confronting these pivotal and crucial institutions. We need to insist on a transformation of relations within our schools, to humanize them; we have to insist upon and facilitate the formal practice of development education, education for individual development and the global development of humankind. Formal and informal education structures, therefore, need to be one common fundamental theatre for the open conspiracy.

As I stated above, however, what people learn and do is not dependent merely upon schools, or on parenting, major and pervasive influences as these are. All social structures – business, commerce, law, medicine, national and international politics, community and social services, information and cultural media, along with education and parenting – need to be transformed. Michel Foucault asserts that in challenging power and oppression, we should not focus merely on state apparatus and ideologies but, rather, on 'domination' and the localized 'techniques and tactics of domination', which includes those officials and functionaries who actually carry out the exercise of power (the 'material operators of power'), and the specific manifestations of this power: the 'forms' of subjection, the 'inflection of localized systems', and the strategic apparatus. And it is those of us who are currently immersed in these structures, as people who provide or receive services, or sanctions, who have to begin this task – where we are.[5]

What needs to be done at every specific locale of such structures, and in their generalized ground, is the open, unequivocal assertion of a humanist radical ethic, in that we neither carry out nor accept – as workers or consumers – decisions, processes or practices that disallow the integrity, dignity, self-esteem, authority, health, growth and creativity of any person, or people. It is necessary that all of us, in our chosen areas – as workers, consumers and citizen activists – propose, promote and assert *new* practices based in open, democratic structures and processes; in equal and shared power, advantage, responsibility and privilege among all persons and peoples; in full and direct access to information and ideas; in active encouragement of intensive public knowledge about, and critique of, social structures; and in assistance to those who wish to promote and participate in the transformation of such structures.

In the context of a mutual support mechanism such as the reference and action groups I have described, and the normative structure of a growing open conspiracy, such a transformation of ourselves and our world can begin. It will not be easy, and the task will not be finished in our lifetime, or even that of our children. But a beginning can be made, and the journey started. What is involved will be long and difficult, rife with pain, trauma and fatigue. The way will be one of constant risk and hazard. But it will also be a journey taken with others, as a mutual celebration of life and awareness – a journey marked by fulfilment, change, and many moments of great joy. This is the promise of our commitment to conspire – to breathe together and act together – to create a more beautiful, humane and just world.

Notes

1. Thomas Kuhn, *The Structure of Scientific Revolutions* (1962). Recent revisionist attacks on Kuhn's treatise from within the inner sanctum of the scientific establishment – and in particular on the application of his theory to the social and political realm – are polemic, not philosophy, and certainly not science (see, for example, Stephen Weinberg, 'The Revolution that Didn't Happen', *New York Review*, 8 October 1998). These attacks need to be interpreted in the context of the intense ideological reaction from both Left and Right to the increasing cultural and political influence of poststructuralist and postmodernist ethics and epistemology. This attack now extends even to Kuhn, because his writing has been one of the inspirations and influences on poststructuralist thinking, and lends it credence and respectability, even though Kuhn (who died in the mid-1990s) never described himself as a postmodernist, and was apparently critical of what he saw as excesses and sloppiness in some postmodernist rhetoric and methods.

2. R.L. Warren, 'Sociology of Knowledge and Problems of the Inner Cities', *Social Science Quarterly*, vol. 52, no. 3, p. 470.

3. Ibid., p. 471.

4. Kuhn, *The Structure of Scientific Revolutions*, p. 6.

5. See Michel Foucault, 'Two Lectures', in *Power/Knowledge: Selected Interviews and Other Writings, 1972-1977*, ed. Colin Gordon (1980), pp. 79-109.

Conclusion

The first words of R.D. Laing's *The Politics of Experience* (1967) are:

> Few books today are forgivable. Black on canvas, silence on the screen, an empty white sheet of paper, are perhaps feasible. There is little conjunction of truth and social 'reality'.

What I have offered in this book is not enough. Our times demand more. I do not believe we have more to give at this time. The mechanisms I have suggested are the most radical available, as they touch the roots of the human psyche, and human practice, and it is the roots that must be transformed if we are to transform ourselves and our social practice, and ultimately change the world.

Unless we act from the basis of individual health, we cannot create a new and truly human world. This is a hard lesson, and those faced with the barbaric inhumanity of repressive regimes and soulless corporations may feel that it is a reactionary one, removed from the hard necessities of the 'material reality' of economic and political relations. I understand this view, but I cannot accede to it. We will learn more as we create our future.

Others will say that what I offer in this book is 'idealistic', that it is grandiose, that I presume a capacity for altruism and change and growth that has no basis in human reality. They will argue that the evils of the modern world are natural conditions of human existence, and that these evils can be mediated only by systematic, rational use of power, coercion and constraint, including the curtailment of individuality and personal freedom for the higher good of stability and the modest improvement of material well-being for at least a plurality within society. This is the classic utilitarian position.

Those who hold this view will insist that what is suggested in this book is not possible. I can only respond that the possible is not an objective fact, but a subjective one. It is our view of what is possible and impossible that is the most critical limit on what actually is possible. I have tried in this book to challenge the conventional and dominant view that the evils of human society are 'natural'. If I only provoke slight debate around this particular ideological lie, I will consider the effort worthwhile.

I have also attempted to show that the individual social practice described here is *not* rooted in simple altruism. To the contrary, human practice is firmly and incontrovertibly rooted in individual self-interest. And because of the essence of our humanity – our humanness – this self-interest strives towards a physical, psychological, intellectual, spiritual and artistic affinity kinship with others.[1] I have also tried to show that – contrary to the conventional fatalist view of human potential – change and growth are not only possible for human individuals and societies; they are the norm. The capacity for self-directed growth and change defines our humanness. It is only through tapping these essential qualities that we will survive.

Those who believe that 'the masses are a great beast', and that societal control is the only means to national survival and progress, pride themselves on the notion that they are 'realists'. If they were to examine reality, they would see two things: that the global human reality at the end of the twentieth century cannot persist; and that the qualities which can move us from this reality to another are exactly those qualities that are most obvious in human beings, and which the powerful most fear and deny because they cannot be controlled. They will fear that the vision presented here can only produce anarchy, decay and the breakdown of society. This fear is an obvious insanity in the face of the anarchy, decay and global breakdown that we are currently experiencing, a breakdown that can be clearly traced to autocratic and totalitarian structures, and the cruel abuse of power. If we do not learn this, we will not create our future, but will merely be its final victims.

The two responses dealt with above are easily anticipated. They have represented the historical poles of national and global political struggle for over two hundred years. And although the second has enjoyed a brief and temporary ascendancy for the last two decades – an ascendancy tragicomically announced as 'the end of history' by triumphantalist acolytes of capitalism – there is no doubt that we are again about to enter a period of intense revolutionary activity against the hegemony of transnational global capital and its political proxies around the world.

There is a third response that I anticipate to this book, and it is a response that concerns me much more deeply than the first two. While the orientations discussed above dominate the ebb and flow of formal politics, the conflicting orientations are, in fact, ardently held by a relatively minuscule proportion of the people affected by them. The vast majority of us are locked into another orientation entirely, and it is the one upon which we must focus. There are too many of us who will say that, really, *nothing* is possible. This is the response I have tried to deal with in this book. And there are many who will not be convinced.

We are all prisoners of the world, and of the conditions of this life. But we are also prisoners of our psychology and our imagination – and so is the world. I believe that if we are indeed fated, then we, and the world, are victims of the imposed limits of our own psychology and imagination. The world is *our* victim, and we with it; we are not the victims of a cruel world.

There is not much more I can say to those who respond with hopelessness. When we deal with our hopelessness, however, we will do well to remember that we in the North *and* South who are among the small affluent minority on this globe not only hold ourselves prisoner, we also hold billions of others prisoner. These are the billions living powerless and poor not only in the so-called Third World, but at the core of the industrialized societies as well – the hidden poor who are our neighbours, and upon whose backs we make our soft and bitter bed. We hold billions prisoner to the limits of our psychology and imagination, and seal the fate of humankind, because, quite literally, it is only through our own radical trans-formation, and the transformations we effect in the structures and practices which provide and maintain our affluent comfort, that a fundamental transformation of the conditions of all humankind can begin.

This is our challenge. The choice is ours, and only ours, and the decision we make is a decision for all humankind – it is a decision to work to ensure that others have the choice that is now our agony and our joy, to ensure that others have the choice to participate in life as well as death, in celebration as well as mourning, to ensure that others may share in the creation of the future of humanity, whether it be dusk or a new dawn.

And above all that decision is, and can only be, a solitary, individual decision: to live, to choose, to act: 'to walk with the others/ And in the end – with time and luck – to dance.'

Note

1. I am speaking here in a ontological sense rather than a biological sense; this position should not be confused with that of socio-biologists such as E.O. Wilson, whose perspectives are antithetical to the ethos of this book.

Epilogue

Eclectic Notes on
Knowledge and Action

This epilogue offers a range of short reflections — some taken from my personal journal written over several years as an activist, others from writers who have influenced my praxis — each of which is an interlude or a vignette that resonates with the ethical and aesthetic impulse that drives this book. These 'eclectic notes' have been selected and arranged almost as a prose poem that frames the essence of this book. The reflections were originally compiled and arranged for an exercise I use to introduce seminars that discuss some of the dilemmas explored in this book. Those written by myself are in ordinary script, while quotes from others are in quotation marks.

- The challenge in life is not to find truths to live by, which are legion, but to choose among them.

- From Canadian activist and Chemistry Nobel laureate John Polanyi:

  'I am thought once to have had an idea. But now I talk about them. There is an important moral to this, namely that ideas are scarce.'

- From Gore Vidal:

  'It is the spirit of the age to believe that any fact, no matter how suspect, is superior to any imaginative exercise, no matter how true.'

- From John Ralston Saul, in *The Unconscious Civilization*:

  'Knowledge is more effectively used today to justify wrong being done, than to prevent it.'

- The willingness and capacity to lie, to lie big, is perhaps the most powerful weapon in the arsenal of oppression and injustice. All those with wealth and power gained their advantage, and sustain this advantage, by lying to those without wealth and power, who they will not allow to lie. The official role of the politician and the bureaucrat is to tell lies and conceal the truth.

- The Lie: power over what is remembered, and what is forgotten.

- From Milan Kundera:

'The struggle of man against power, is the struggle of memory against forgetting.'

- And a related observation:

'The world always makes the assumption that the exposure of an error is identical with the discovery of the truth – that error and truth are simply opposite. They are nothing of the sort. What the world turns to, when it has been cured of one error, is usually simply another error, and maybe one worse than the first one.' (H.L. Mencken)

- From Latin American social analyst Hector Dada (quoted in *Envio*, August 1995):

'Democracy is confrontation to achieve compromise. Totalitarian systems are the ones that require social harmony without fissures.'

- We spend our lives talking to ourselves. One long conversation, the most meaningful and profound we will ever have. If we cannot talk well to ourselves, there is little hope for our intercourse with others.

- The essence, the purpose of life, is to transcend the circumstances of our birth.

- From Martin Carter, poet and activist from Guyana:

'we who want true poems
must all be born again, and die to do so.'

- In Quito airport, decaying and dirty, 6 a.m.: grabbing the daily Air Ecuatoriana milk-run to Miami. I saw a fat, rich man, assured and scaly, with slick hair and oily skin. He knew his place, and others knew theirs. He occupied a vast space which others entered only when invited, and with deference to the ominous power which exuded from him. A liar's smile formed his mouth, but never reached his cold eyes. I thought: in a country of the poor, like this one, a man who is rich is a thief, and the thief must kill to gather his riches. This man was a thief and a killer – and he was travelling First Class.

• Bob Dylan: 'To live outside the law you must be honest.'

• Images in my mind as I leave Colombia, recorded in my journal:
  – murderers on motorcycles
  – the beautiful Magdelena river
  – the tree of life and the poor people of *barrio* Boston
  – the bullet-pocked porch of the café in Pablo Acuna
  – Monica's dignity in her tiny shack
  – the peaceful mountains on the way to San Vincente
  – the faces of the soldiers surrounding the village hall in San Vincente
  – the despair of the old couple we met at the human rights office, who had been driven from their home and land because their sons had joined the guerrillas
  – the whispered reactions each time the people we met learned of another assassination
  – my tired face in the mirror, wondering whether I recognized myself any more ...

• From Russell Banks, *Continental Drift*:

'We are the planet, fully as much as its water, earth, fire and air are the planet, and if the planet survives it will only be through heroism. Not occasional heroism, a remarkable instance of it here and there, but constant heroism, systematic heroism, heroism as governing principle.'

• From Marge Piercy, 'The Low Road' (in *The Moon is Always Female*, 1980):

'Two people can keep each other
sane, can give support, conviction,
love, massage, hope, sex.
Three people are a delegation
a committee, a wedge. With six
you can rent a whole house,
eat pie for dinner with no
seconds, and hold a fund-raising party.
A dozen make a demonstration.
A hundred fill a hall.

A thousand have solidarity and your own newsletter;
ten thousand, power and your own paper;
a hundred thousand, your own media;
ten million, your own country.
It goes on one at a time,
it starts when you care
to act, it starts when you do
it again after they said no,
it starts when you say WE
and know who you mean, and each
day you mean one more.'

* From *An Imaginary Life*, by David Malouf:

'But we are free after all. We are bound not by the laws of our nature but
by the ways we can imagine ourselves breaking out of those laws without
doing violence to our essential being. We are free to transcend ourselves.
If we have the imagination for it.'

* A reflection, 'On Literacy', which I wrote in dissent to mark International Literacy Year (1990):

Literacy is not language. Speaking and listening are language.
Literacy is not reading and writing. Reading and writing are tools: they
are merely one technology of language, and one tool of the literate.
Literacy is essentially private. It is a private link to the public world.
The tools of literacy are psycho-social tools. They are devices of the
interior.
Literacy allows the individual to interiorize, over space and time, the
socialized experience of others; and to socialize, over space and time,
one's own interior experiences. Literacy is the link between inner space
and outer space. Literacy allows the individual to transcend space and
time altogether.
Literacy cannot be given nor taken, taught nor learned. It is not a skill,
it is a *quality of being*.
If a person is marginalized, offering literacy will not diminish this
marginalization. If a person does not read and write, teaching reading and
writing will not allow her to read and write.
The essence of literacy is not language, but *participation*. Language is a
medium of participation, and a medium of experience.
A person without participation is a person without literacy. Her experience is solitary and asocial. Everyone participates in the world to some
extent; to that extent, they are literate.
All persons have some literacy. There are no 'illiterates'.

Literacy is participation. Only participation can develop a person's literacy:
- social literacy develops with *social participation*;
- political literacy develops with *political participation*;
- economic literacy develops with *economic participation*;
- cultural literacy develops with *cultural participation*.

Job literacy develops through meaningful and dignified work, and educational literacy develops with positive learning experiences, and civil literacy develops with humane and responsible interaction with authority. And so on...

The quality of participation determines the quality of literacy. And literacy is merely a quality of social existence: where the interior being meets the world, where the private and the public embrace.

Literacy is not the product of a process, nor the means to an end. It is not the problem, and it is not the solution.

To enhance literacy is to enhance the quality of social existence – to enhance, that is, the degree and quality of social participation.

To enhance literacy is to engage with the marginalized: socially, politically, economically, culturally. It is to accompany the marginal, participate with them in their bruised and shy prodigal tug at the hem of a neglectful society.

What is *not* needed are programs that seek to change the victims of society, but that leave society as it is. To advertise literacy programs to the disadvantaged on the promise that this is a way out of the maze of social and economic isolation is a lie, and malicious fraud.

- From Michael Ignatieff, *The Needs of Strangers*:

'a decent and humane society requires a shared language of the good. The one our society lives by – a language of rights – has no terms for the dimensions of the human good which require acts of virtue unspecifiable as a legal or civil obligation.'

'It is as common for us to need things on behalf of others, to need good schools for the sake of our children, safe streets for the sake of our neighbours, decent old people's homes for the strangers at our door, as it is to need them for ourselves. The deepest motivational springs of political involvement are to be located in this human capacity to feel needs for others.'

- From Susan Sontag, *On Style* (1965):

'Art is connected to morality, I should argue. One way that it is so connected is that art may yield moral pleasure; but the moral pleasure peculiar to art is not the pleasure of approving of acts or disapproving of them. The moral pleasure in art, as well as the moral service that art performs, consists in the intelligent gratification of consciousness.'

- Later she expands on this theme:

  'An approach which considers works of art as living autonomous models of consciousness will seem objectionable only so long as we refuse to surrender the shallow distinction of form and content. For the sense in which a work of art has no content is no different than the sense in which the world has no content. Both are. Both need no justification; nor could they possibly have any … the world (all there is) cannot, ultimately be justified. Justification is an operation of the mind which can be performed only when we consider one part of the world in relation to another – not when we consider all there is.'

- And from *The Aesthetics of Silence* (1967):

  'The history of art is a sequence of successful transgressions.'

- From a letter by the author to an activist friend:

  Is there really anything about organized society and the way it actually works in the world today to justify the political notion of 'grassroots'? A few scattered alternative groups, even those 'based in community', are not a grassroots, and do not constitute a movement. I believe that this phrase has become part of our cant, and blinds us to the limits of our work, and the tremendous challenges that lie ahead for us if we are serious in our articulated role to promote fundamental change. If we really want to change things, at least in a hundred years, we may have to revise our perspectives and create new metaphors which are more accurate and useful, and come out of our real experience. Because, concerning fundamental change, I really don't believe that we can get there from here.

- Some things never change; *these* are the things which we should most relentlessly focus upon as change agents.

- From *The Victorian House*, by Philip Child:

  'But the prose we live is not the poetry
  We write in what we think are times of insight
  When the rhythm of thought is fluctuant and swift,
  And the merging of arrested glance with love,
  Of spark and fire, can come to pass between
  The falling of two motes of dust to the floor,
  Or between two beats of the heart – so swift it is.
  The daily prose is coarser, tougher; its bricks
  Are glazed with indifference and mortared with boredom;
  We built its walls to surround the Debate in the Soul
  And resist the remorseless probing of the rats;
  We would not open the door to every knock

Of a stranger.
It is not true that every breath
I breathe is breathed in prayer of those I love…'

• From a letter to an activist friend:

There are many ideas, but all of this presumes that people are not sceptical about the possibility that something better could be done than we
are doing now. The *Titanic* analogy – the accusation that we only wish to
rearrange the deckchairs – is a perverse cliché, bloated with hidden assumptions, and blighted with apocalyptic negative fantasy. Our 'ship' has
not hit an iceberg; it is merely run aground. It is not going to sink, but
neither is it going to move. So rearranging the deckchairs (and much of
the other furniture) actually isn't such a silly exercise; however, it's not
enough, and anyway, it has already been done.

Rather, what *is* necessary is to realize that our ship isn't a ship any
more; it's an *island*. And we aren't passengers and sailors; we are *islanders*.
And we are going to have to live here for a long, long time, cohabiting
with this finite space. So we had better stop trying to refit a ship, and
recognize that the skills of sailors are not appropriate; and start to
accommodate ourself to living on an island, and develop the skills that
islanders need.

Shifting the analogy like this is what I meant by asking new questions,
and creating 'discontinuities'. Between a ship at sea, and a remote and
deserted island, there is an absolute discontinuity, which is why the adventures of Robinson Crusoe and the Swiss Family Robinson were so
compelling to millions of readers (and certainly more compelling than the
bizarre travesty of the *Titanic*, a mere obscenity of human arrogance and
error, and not even a very good story, let alone a useful analogy for
human dilemmas as we approach the millennium).

The theme of *sustainability* is key … whether about avoiding dupli-
cation, or promoting a new generation of leadership, or about tinkering
with a failed model, an obsolete idea (a doomed ship …), or about
'reinventing the wheel'. If we all didn't have to start from scratch perhaps
all this would not be necessary, but when you suddenly find yourself on
an island without a user's manual, the first thing you have to do is re-
invent the wheel.

• From Norbert Wiener, in *The Human Use of Human Beings*:

'It is quite conceivable that life belongs to a limited stretch of time; that
before the earliest geological ages it did not exist, and that the time may
well come when the earth is again a lifeless, burnt-out, or frozen planet.
To those of us who are aware of the extremely limited range of human
conditions under which the chemical reactions necessary to life as we
know it can take place, it is a foregone conclusion that the lucky accident

which permits the continuation of life in any form on this earth, even without restricting life to something like human life, is bound to come to a complete and disastrous end. Yet we may succeed in framing our values so that this temporary accident of living existence, and this more temporary accident of human existence, may be taken as all-important positive values, notwithstanding their fugitive character.

In a very real sense, we are shipwrecked passengers on a doomed planet. Yet even in a shipwreck, human decencies and human values do not necessarily vanish, and we must make the most of them. We shall go down, but let it be in a manner to which we may look forward as worthy of our dignity.'

- From Fritjof Capra, quoted by Ursula Le Guin (in *A Non-Euclidean View of California*, 1982):

'The activities of a machine are determined by its structure, but the relation is reversed in organisms – organic structure is determined by its processes.'

- Le Guin herself points out:

'It seems fairly clear to me that to count on technological advance for anything but technological advance is a mistake.'

- Piaget said: 'to learn is to invent'. He believed that people do not learn by acquisition, by being 'taught' what others 'know', but that each individual develops understanding only by inventing knowledge anew, personally. There is considerable evidence that the same is true for people-in-groups, in community. It is not the wheel that is important – it is the invention. And it is not the answer that is important, but the question itself, and that the answer is invented by the person who originally asked the question. Only thus will the answers be applicable in real-life situations; and only thus will arise *new* questions.

- From a letter to an activist friend:

Power is centralized and controlled in all societies through a system that assures that there are privileged people who have all the 'answers' (which are the real collateral and capital in any society), and who also make up the questions. The answers come first; the questions are there merely to justify and verify the revealed answers. The keepers of knowledge program the questions to seek only the prescribed answers, thereby assuring their privilege and power. Anyone posing new questions, or questions that the elect cannot answer, is marginalized, censored, and often obliterated. The one who can pose even one new question that successfully engages the consciousness and imagination of the populace, undermines prevailing power and, momentarily at least, creates the possibility of revolution.

- From an essay on beauty and truth by Mindy Aloff:

  'Far more fundamental to a theory's beauty than an uncomplicated proof is the simplicity of its basic ideas.... Elegance, like intelligence, breeds admiration. Simplicity, like depth of human feeling, stimulates conviction and love.... And by 'simplicity', I mean something particular – not simplemindedness, not minimalism, not utilitarian geometry, not stripped-down style. I mean emotional and spiritual integrity ... I mean a quality that, if one is open to it, may be apprehended with the speed of feeling, regardless of the degree of elaboration.'

- From Boris Pasternak: 'The root of beauty is audacity.'

- From Bertolt Brecht, *The World's One Hope*:

  'The more there are suffering, then the more natural their sufferings appear. Who wants to prevent the fishes from getting wet? And the suffering themselves share this callousness towards themselves and are lacking kindness towards themselves. It is terrible that human beings so easily put up with existing conditions, not only with the suffering of strangers but also their own. All those who have thought about the bad state of things refuse to appeal to the compassion of one group of people for another. But the compassion of the oppressed for the oppressed is indispensable. It is the world's one hope.'

- From Chinua Achebe, *Anthills of the Savannah*:

  'There is no universal conglomerate of the oppressed. Free people may be alike everywhere in their freedom, but the oppressed inhabit each their own peculiar hell. The present orthodoxies of deliverance are futile to the extent that they fail to recognize this.'

- From Francis Ponge, in *The Silent World Is Our Only Homeland*:

  'It could be said that the very beauty of the world is what makes life so difficult for us. Did I say difficult? Beauty is the impossible which lasts. We have everything to say ... and can say nothing; that is why we begin anew each day, on the widest variety of subjects and in the greatest number of imaginable procedures....

  The silent world is our only homeland. We make use of its possibilities according to the needs of our times.'

- From Eduardo Galeano, from *The Book of Embraces*:

  'Why does one write, if not to put one's pieces together? From the moment we enter school or church, education chops us into pieces: it teaches us to divorce soul from body and mind from heart. The fisher-men off the Colombian coast must be learned doctors of ethics and morality, for they invented the word *sentipensante*, feeling-thinking, to de-fine language that speaks the truth.'

'Turn loose the voices, undream the dreams ... In these countries ... every promise is a threat, every loss a discovery. Courage is born of fear, certainty of doubt. Dreams announce the possibility of another reality, and out of the delirium emerges another kind of reason.

What it comes down to is that we are the sum of our efforts to change who we are. Identity is no museum piece sitting stock-still in a display case, but rather the endlessly astonishing synthesis of the contra-dictions of everyday life.'

'There is just one place where yesterday and today meet, recognize each other, and embrace, and that place is tomorrow.'

- And from Montesquieu: 'A really intelligent person feels what others only know.'

- A reflection on balance, from my journal:

Freedom avoids the traps set by the world;
Wisdom goes further, and avoids the traps we set for ourselves.
It is the struggle that honours us, not the victory.
Friendship is struggle shared, and needs no laurels...

- Another fragment, this from Imamu Amiri Baraka, in his *Political Poem*:

Luxury, then, is a way of
being ignorant, comfortably.
An approach to the open market
of least information. Where theories
can thrive, under heavy tarpaulins
without being cracked by ideas.

- From the Argentinean Ricardo Piglia, in *Artificial Respiration*:

'Against himself, always against himself ... that method seemed to him an almost infallible guarantee of lucidity. They train us for so long to be stupid and finally it becomes second nature to us.... "The first thing we think is always mistaken", he would say, "it's a conditioned reflex".'

Another resonance from Piglia, not unconnected: 'I prefer, he said, being a failure to being an accomplice.'

- More from John Ralston Saul, in *The Unconscious Civilization*:

  ‘"We know the good," Euripides wrote, "but do not practice it." The true characteristic of consciousness is therefore not simply knowledge, but a balanced use of our qualities so that what we know and say is related to what we do.’

  ‘The corporate system depends on the citizen’s desire for inner comfort. Equilibrium is dependent upon our recognition of reality, which is the acceptance of permanent psychic discomfort. And the acceptance of psychic discomfort is the acceptance of consciousness.’

- From Rollo May, in *Love and Will*:

  ‘Thus, the crisis in will does not arise from either the presence or absence of power in the individual’s world. It comes from the contradiction between the two – the result of which is a paralysis of will.’

- And again from Rollo May, this time from *Power and Innocence*:

  ‘there is no meaningful "yes" unless the individual could also have said "no". Consciousness requires the exercise of the individual’s counterwill; it is called forth, inspired, and developed, by the conflicts that occur in every individual’s life which force [her] to call on power that [she] did not know [she] possessed.’

- From Susan Freilicher:

  ‘Dreamwalker’s heart is in the south … brings the medicine of passion and creativity into our lives. She asks us to remember when our lives held promise and passion, when life was so exciting that our hearts beat like the pounding of horses’ hooves. She dares us to expect our dreams and fantasies to become reality. She brings us the medicine of our own potential.’

- A few reflections from another trip jotted in my journal:

  – When people wear a disguise too long, they become what they pretend to be.
  – The simple battery defies the notion that energy cannot be created. Is there an analogy here for political organizing? The elements arranged, the point of contact, the focus, and energy revealed in light, movement, and sound: the static transformed. This is not creating anything that was not there before. It is simply vision, insight and ‘arrangement’ of the static to create movement. Similarly, by analogy, when the cynic says that there is nothing – nothing to do, nothing to work with – he is simply

trapped in the immobility before movement, the silence before sound, the darkness before the light. The visionary sees what is, in what is not.

   – An analogy that struck me during a conversation with the organizers in La Libertad: it is the tiniest spring and the most modest stream that eventually turn the waterwheel, and the turbine. If each spring and stream knew this, they would experience the power of mighty rivers. Successful movements teach the source what rivers know.

• Finally, in *The Sheltering Sky*, Paul Bowles quotes Kafka:

'From a certain point onward there is no longer any turning back. That is the point that must be reached.'

Related Reading

Arendt, Hannah, *The Human Condition*, University of Chicago Press, Chicago, 1958.

Alinsky, Saul, *Rules for Radicals*, Random House, New York, 1971.

Bremer, John, *A Matrix for Modern Education*, McClelland & Stewart, Toronto, 1975.

Bronowski, Jacob, *Science and Human Values,* Harper & Row, New York, 1956, 1965 (revised).

Bronowski, Jacob, *The Identity of Man*, Natural History Press (Doubleday), Garden City NY, 1965, 1971 (revised).

Bronowski, Jacob, *The Ascent of Man*, Little, Brown, Boston MA, 1973.

Buber, Martin, *I and Thou*, Scribner, New York, 1970.

Camus, Albert, *The Rebel*, trans. Anthony Bower, Vintage, New York, 1956.

Chomsky, Noam, *Problems of Knowledge and Freedom*, Random House, New York, 1971.

Chomsky, Noam, and Edward S. Herman, *Manufacturing Consent*, Pantheon, New York, 1988.

Darby, Tom (ed.), *Sojourns in the New World, Reflections on Technology*, Carleton University, Ottawa, 1986.

Derrida, Jacques, *Specters of Marx*, trans. Peggy Kamuf, Routledge, New York, 1994.

Duesberg, Peter H., with Bryan J. Ellison, *Inventing the AIDS Virus*, Regnery, Washington DC, 1996.

Duncan, Ronald, and Miranda Weston-Smith (eds), *The Encyclopedia of Ignorance*, Simon & Schuster, New York, 1978.

Fanon, Frantz, *The Wretched of the Earth*, trans. Constance Farrington, Grove Press, New York, 1968.

Faure, Edgar, et al., *Learning to Be: The World of Education Today and Tomorrow*, UNESCO/Harrap, London, 1972.

Feyerabend, Paul, *Against Method*, Verso, London, 1975, 1993 (3rd revised edn).

Forcé, Carolyn, *Twentieth Century Poetry of Witness*, Norton, New York, 1993.

Foucault, Michel, *Power/Knowledge: Selected Interviews and Other Writings 1972–77*, ed. Colin Gordon, Pantheon, New York, 1980.

Fowles, John, *The Aristos*, New American Library, Boston MA, 1970.

Frankl, Victor, *Man's Search for Meaning*, Beacon Press, Boston MA, 1959.

Freire, Paulo, *Pedagogy of the Oppressed*, Herder & Herder, New York, 1972.

Freire, Paulo, *Education for Critical Consciousness*, Seabury, New York, 1973

Fromm, Erich, *Escape from Freedom*, Avon, New York, 1941, 1965.

Fromm, Erich, *The Sane Society*, Fawcett, Greenwich CT, 1955.

Fromm, Erich, *The Heart of Man*, Harper & Row, New York, 1964.

Galeano, Eduardo, *The Book of Embraces*, trans. Cedric Belfrage, W.W. Norton, New York, 1991.

Galeano, Eduardo, *Days and Nights of Love and War*, trans. Judith Brister, Monthly Review Press, New York, 1983.

George, Jim, *Discourses of Global Politics: A Critical (Re)Introduction to International Relations*, Lynne Rienner, Boulder CO, 1994.

Gilligan, Carol, *In a Different Voice*, Harvard University Press, Cambridge MA, 1982.

Goodman, Paul, *Growing Up Absurd*, Vintage, New York, 1960.

Gramsci, Antonio, *Selections from the Prison Notebooks*, trans. Quintin Hoare and Geoffrey Nowell Smith, International Publishers, New York, 1971.

Grant, George, *Technology and Empire*, Anansi, Toronto, 1969.

Hawking, Stephen, *A Brief History of Time*, Bantam, New York, 1988.

Heilbroner, Robert, *Teachings from the Worldly Philosophy*, Norton, New York, 1996.

Hobsbawm, E.J., *The Age of Extremes: A History of the World 1914–91*, Pantheon, New York, 1994.

hooks, bell, *Feminist Theory: From Margin to Center*, South End Press, Boston MA, 1984.

Hoyle, Fred, *Ten Faces of the Universe*, Heinemann, London, 1977.

Huntington, Samuel, *The Clash of Civilizations and the New World Order*, Simon & Schuster, New York, 1996, 1998.

Ignatieff, Michael, *The Needs of Strangers*, Penguin, Harmondsworth, 1984, 1986.

Illich, Ivan, *Celebration of Awareness*, Introduction by Erich Fromm, Doubleday, New York, 1970.

Kaplan, Robert, 'The Coming Anarchy', *Atlantic Monthly*, November 1994, pp. 44–76.

Kuhn, Thomas, *The Structure of Scientific Revolutions*, University of Chicago, Chicago, 1970 (2nd edn).

Laing, R.D., *The Divided Self*, Penguin, Harmondsworth, 1960.

Laing, R.D., *The Politics of Experience*, Penguin, Harmondsworth, 1967.

Laszlo, Ervin, *The Creative Cosmos*, Floris, Edinburgh, 1993.

Lauritsen, John, *The AIDS War*, ASKLEPIOS, New York, 1993.

Lewontin, R.C., *The Genetic Basis for Evolutionary Change*, Columbia University Press, New York, 1974.

Lewontin, R.C., *Biology as Ideology*, Anansi, Toronto, 1991.

Lewontin, R.C., S. Rose and L.J. Kamin, *Not in our Genes*, Pantheon, New York, 1984.

McLuhan, Marshall, *Understanding Media: The Extensions of Man*, McGraw-Hill, New York, 1965; reissued with an introduction by Lewis Lapham, MIT Press, Cambridge MA, 1994.

Marcuse, Herbert, *One-Dimensional Man: Studies in the Ideology of Advanced Industrial Society*, Beacon Press, Boston MA, 1964.

Marcuse, Herbert, *Counter-Revolution and Revolt*, Beacon Press, Boston MA, 1972.

Maslow, Abraham, *Toward a Psychology of Being*, Van Nostrand Reinhold, New York, 1968 (2nd edn).

Maslow, Abraham, *The Farthest Reaches of Human Nature*, Penguin, Harmondsworth, 1972, 1976.

May, Rollo, *Man's Search for Himself*, Dell, New York, 1953.

May, Rollo, *Love and Will*, Dell, New York, 1969.

May, Rollo, *Power and Innocence*, Norton, New York, 1972.

Miller, Jean Baker, *Toward a New Psychology of Women*, Beacon Press, Boston MA, 1976.

Murphy, Brian K., 'El Salvador: A Canadian Looks in the Mirror', *Canadian Dimension*, vol. 20, no. 6, November 1986, pp. 28–32.

Murphy, Brian K., 'Waiting for the Apocalypse', *Canadian Forum*, vol. LXVIII, no. 782, October 1989, pp. 31–2.

Murphy, Brian K., 'The Dice are Loaded (Structural Adjustment and the Poor)', *Canadian Forum*, vol. LXIX, no. 794, November 1990, pp. 12–17.

Murphy, Brian K., 'Canadian NGOs and the Politics of Participation', in Jamie Swift and Brian Tomlinson (eds), *Conflicts of Interests, Canada and the Third World*, Between The Lines, Toronto, 1991, pp. 161–212.

Murphy, Brian K., 'The Politics of AIDS', *Third World Resurgence*, no. 47, July 1994, pp. 33–40.

Murphy, Brian K., 'AIDS Obscures Injustice and Medicalizes Poverty', *Canadian Dimension*, vol. 29, no. 3, June/July 1995, pp. 38–46.

National Anti-Poverty Organization (NAPO), *A Human Rights Meltdown in Canada: Submission to the U.N. Committee On Economic, Social and Cultural Rights*, NAPO, Ottawa/Geneva, November 1998.

Pearce, Joseph Chilton, *The Crack in the Cosmic Egg*, Julien Press, New York, 1971.

Pettman, Jan Jindy, *Worlding Women: A Feminist International Politics*, Routledge, New York, 1996.

Piaget, Jean, *To Understand is to Invent: The Future of Education*, Penguin, Harmondsworth, 1976.

Pilger, John, *Heroes*, Pan, London, 1986.

Pilger, John, *Hidden Agendas*, Vintage, London, 1998.

Postman, Neil, and Charles Weingartner, *Teaching as a Subversive Activity*, Dell, New York, 1969.

Revel, Jean-François, *Without Marx or Jesus*, Dell, New York, 1971.

Revel, Jean-François, *The Totalitarian Temptation*, Penguin, Harmondsworth, 1976.

Robertson, James, *The Sane Alternative*, Villiers, London, 1978.

Rogers, Carl, *On Becoming a Person*, Houghton Mufflin, Boston MA, 1961.

Rogers, Carl, *Freedom to Learn*, C.E. Merrill, Columbus OH, 1969.

Root-Bernstein, Robert, *Rethinking AIDS: The Tragic Cost of Premature Consensus*, The Free Press/Macmillan, New York, 1993.

Rose, Hilary, *Love, Power and Knowledge: Towards a Feminist Transformation of the Sciences*, Indiana University Press, Bloomington, 1994.

Rosak, Theodore, *Where the Wasteland Ends*, Doubleday, New York, 1973.

Sagan, Carl, *The Cosmic Connection*, Dell, New York, 1973.

Sagan, Carl, *The Dragons of Eden*, Random House, New York, 1977.

Sagan, Carl, *Broca's Brain*, Random House, New York, 1979.

Saul, John Ralston, *The Unconscious Civilization*, Anansi, Toronto, 1995.

Selye, Hans, *Stress without Distress*, New American Library, New York, 1974.

Selye, Hans, *The Stress of Life*, McGraw-Hill, New York, 1996 (revised edn).

Sheldrake, Rupert, *The Presence of the Past*, Park Street Press, Rochester VT, 1988, 1995.

Shenton, Joan, *Positively False: Exposing the Myths around HIV and AIDS*, I.B. Tauris and St Martin's Press, London and New York, 1998.

Sontag, Susan, *A Susan Sontag Reader*, ed. Elizabeth Hardwick, Farrar, Straus & Giroux, New York, 1982.

Sontag, Susan, *AIDS and its Metaphors*, Farrar, Straus & Giroux, New York, 1989, 1989.

Teilhard De Chardin, Pierre, *The Phenomenon of Man*, trans. Bernard Wall, Collins, London, 1959, 1970 (revised edn).

UNDP, *Human Development Report 1998*, United Nations/Oxford University Press, Oxford and New York, 1998.

Waldby, Catherine, *Aids and the Body Politic: Biomedicine and Sexual Difference*, Routledge, London and New York, 1996.

Warren, R.L. 'Sociology of Knowledge and Problems of the Inner City', *Social Science Quarterly*, vol. 52, no. 3, 1971, pp. 469–91.

Weinberg, Stephen, 'The Revolution that Didn't Happen', *New York Review*, 8 October 1998.

Wiener, Norbert, *The Human Use of Human Beings*, Anchor Books/Doubleday, New York, 1954 (2nd revised edn); re-issued by De Capo, New York, 1994.

Index

fantasy, negative, 26
fatalism, 74
Faure, Edgar, 94
Faure Report, 94
feeling, definition of, 45
feminist theory, 34, 60
Feminist Theory: From Margin to Center
(hooks), 39n
Feyerabend, Paul, 99n
foreign policy, US, 9
Foucault, Michel, 27n, 131–2, 133n
Fowles, John, 121n
Freilicher, Susan, 148–9
Freire, Paulo, 10, 78, 81, 98n
Fromm, Erich, 9, 28n, 33–5, 38n
fundamentalism, religious, 24–5
future, embracing, 112–21

Galeano, Eduardo, 35, 146–7
Genetic Basis of Evolutionary Change, The
(Lewontin), 51n
genetic information base, 44
genetic knowledge, 57
genetic mutation, 54
George, Jim, 111n
Gilligan, Carol, 39n
Gödel, Kurt, 58
Gramsci, Antonio, 99n
Grant, George, 51n
group process, in education, 91–2
group/self, 115–18
groups, 54
growth, risk and, 26

Hawking, Stephen, 76n
health
    and action, 113–14
    allies for, 103–10
    definition of, 14–15
    factors of, 15–19
    threats to, 19–23
heroism, 140
Hiroshima, 89
history, linear, 74–6
Hitler, Adolf, 89
HIV, 19, 27n
hopelessness, as response, 14
Human Condition, The (Arendt), 27n, 51n
Human Development Report 1988
    (UNDP), 7, 12n
Human Rights Meltdown in Canada, 12n

Human Use of Human Beings, The
    (Weiner), 27n, 51n, 144–5
humanist radicalism, 9, 33–8
'humanness', 35
Huntington, Samuel, 12n

I and Thou (Buber), 65n
identity, definition of, 16, 63
identity needs, reference group and,
    104
Identity of Man, The (Bronowski), 52,
    65n, 77n
ideological radicalism, 30–3
ideology, 30
Ignatieff, Michael, 27n, 142
Illich, Ivan, 38n, 103, 121n, 131
Imaginary Life, An (Malouf), 41, 141
imagination, 45–6
    in education, 90–91
immutable human nature, established
    rationality and, 71–2
immutable moral law, established
    rationality and, 72–4
imperialism, cultural, 55
In a Different Voice (Gilligan), 39n
Indeterminacy, Principle of, 58
individual, 52–65
    in society, 62–5
individuality, 57
inertia
    beyond, 29–38
    psychology of, 13–26
'insanity' (Marcuse), 10
integration, education and, 86–7
intellect, democracy of, 80–84, 83
intelligence, of human beings, 44
internalizing, stress and, 30
international process, education and, 87
intolerance, institutionalization of, 30
isolation, and activism, 118–21

Kafka, Franz, 149
Kaplan, Robert, 9, 12n
knowledge, 55–60, 57
    limits of, 72
Kuhn, Thomas, 123, 127–9, 133n
Kundera, Milan, 139

Laing, R.D., 27n, 134
language
    limitations of, 73